MI9 AND THE SECRET WAR IN GREECE 1941–1945

THE REMARKABLE STORY OF MAJOR FRANK MACASKIE MC and BAR

MI9 AND THE SECRET WAR IN GREECE 1941–1945

THE REMARKABLE STORY OF MAJOR FRANK MACASKIE MC and BAR

MATTHEW RICHARDSON

Pen & Sword
MILITARY
AN IMPRINT OF PEN & SWORD BOOKS LTD.
YORKSHIRE – PHILADELPHIA

First published in Great Britain in 2026 by
Pen & Sword Military
An imprint of
Pen & Sword Books Ltd
Yorkshire - Philadelphia

ISBN 978 1 03613 641 3

A CIP catalogue record for this book is available from the British Library.

Typeset in INDIA by IMPEC eSolutions
Printed and bound in England by CPI Group (UK) Ltd, Croydon, CRO 4YY

The Publisher's authorised representative in the EU for product safety is Authorised Rep Compliance Ltd., Ground Floor, 71 Lower Baggot Street, Dublin D02 P593, Ireland.
www.arccompliance.com

For a complete list of Pen & Sword titles please contact:

PEN & SWORD BOOKS LIMITED
George House, Units 12 & 13, Beevor Street,
Off Pontefract Road, Barnsley, S71 1HN, UK
E-mail: enquiries@pen-and-sword.co.uk
Website: www.pen-and-sword.co.uk

or

PEN AND SWORD BOOKS
1950 Lawrence Road, Havertown, PA 19083, USA
E-mail: uspen-and-sword@casematepublishers.com
Website: www.penandswordbooks.com

MIX
Paper | Supporting responsible forestry
FSC www.fsc.org
FSC® C013604

Contents

Acknowledgements		vi
Introduction		ix
Chapter One	A Young Man Who Would Fight	1
Chapter Two	A New Diomedes	8
Chapter Three	Greek Adventures	30
Chapter Four	Disaster and Defiance	56
Chapter Five	With MI9 Again	129
Chapter Six	Out of the Shadows?	164
Appendix I: Biographical details of the main Greek protagonists mentioned in the text		179
Appendix II: Significant Greek Resistance Organisations		185
Notes		187
Bibliography		192
Index		194

Acknowledgements

My interest in the remarkable military career of Frank Macaskie really began in 2001, when I was in contact with the late Colonel John Marriott. He had fought alongside Macaskie on Crete, and it was Marriott who first mentioned the name to me as someone who had not only escaped from enemy captivity, but had done so more than once. At that time, he merited only a passing mention in a book that I was writing called *Fighting Tigers*, but Macaskie intrigued me and periodically I returned to his story, gradually adding more details as the years rolled by. More and more it struck me how extraordinary it was that this man was so little known. With a string of exploits to his name, his Military Cross and bar hardly seemed to begin to reflect his achievements. Perhaps it was the fact that he died so tragically young that meant he was not the subject of any war film or TV documentary.

A few years ago, I discovered the memoir *Escape to Nowhere* by Francis Jones. Jones knew Macaskie personally and, I later found out, had tried in the 1970s to produce a book about his friend. He was thwarted however by the fact that at that time many of the necessary documents were still closed. This might have been as far as my research progressed, were it not for the fact that in 2024 two pieces of good fortune came my way. Firstly by happy coincidence I met Dimitris Giannoglou, a military doctor and avid war historian. Dimitris was able to aid me with previously unavailable source material in Greece; indeed it is fair to say that without his knowledge of Greek language texts, the book could not have been completed. The second stroke of luck came when I was able to locate Macaskie's niece. The willingness of the Macaskie family to assist me in this project, with photos, letters and cuttings has been unstinting and I hope that I have through this endeavour both repaid their kindness, and ensured that the memory of their forebear lives on.

Upon commencing the research for the book in earnest, I received more help from a number of sources. Kevin Asplin, whose expertise has underpinned several of my projects in the past, once more worked his magic at the National Archives. Gervald Frykman, the archivist at Warwick School was also generous with his assistance. Marco Grilli, Secretary of the Prefecture at the Vatican Apostolic Archives, likewise offered valuable support. Also in Italy, Professor Amedeo Arena provided much help for which I am grateful. At the Swiss Diplomatic Archives, Yves Steiner provided important assistance. In Edinburgh, John Burnett was an invaluable help at the National Library of Scotland. Raymond Simonds and Rosey Woollcombe provided information about Tony Simonds for which I thank them. Special mention must go to Middlebury College Special Collections, whose archive materials are freely available to the public, as the holders of the letters of Harry Massey, an invaluable resource, likewise Centropa archive is gratefully acknowledged, and the help of Trinity College Dublin library. Linda McGregor at the

Alexander Turnbull Library in New Zealand also provided a generous and speedy response to my request for assistance, as did Tracy Rostron at Manchester Central Library. Anne Wickes at the Second World War Experience Centre was also prompt and helpful in response to my enquiry.

For photographic material, I must gratefully acknowledge the help of Robin Woodbine Parish, for permission to use a photograph belonging to his late father. Dr Natalia Vogeikoff-Brogan, Director of Archives at the American School of Classical Studies Athens also offered help and advice. I am grateful to Hugh Hassard Jones for permission to reproduce the image of Trevor Jones herein, and to Andrew Lovelady for helping with this. To Alexandra Henderson I extend my sincere thanks for permission to reproduce two photographs belonging to her mother Mary Henderson, as well as for advice and guidance. John Caley assisted with software skills, as so often before.

Lastly I must thank the staff of Pen and Sword books, in particular Charles Hewitt and Amy Jordan, for their support and encouragement, not just with this project (though that has been invaluable) but with so many others as well.

Matthew Richardson
Douglas 2025

Introduction

As with so many other young men of his generation, the coming of the Second World War irrevocably changed the direction of Frank Macaskie's life. Before the war he had enjoyed a privileged existence, but his life had also lacked focus. For all its evils, war provided Macaskie with the one thing he had been missing – a purpose. The cause of Greece had never entered his mind before he joined the army, but the thought of the cradle of democracy being ground under the heel of the Nazi jackboot, and the valiant efforts of the Greek people to win back their freedom, stirred in him a sense of romance and adventure. Despite the lack of such inspiration amid the austerity of the post-war world, Macaskie might still have gone on to even greater things, had he not died before his time. This, and the fact that the war in Greece was overshadowed in the eyes of later generations by the drama of Normandy and D-Day, meant that his story was untold for many years.

The book which you are about to read covers not just Macaskie's time in Greece during the war, but also his childhood, his early years as a man, and the violent and destructive campaign in Crete in which he participated with the 2nd Battalion Leicestershire Regiment. It goes on to explore his role in the early stages of the Cold War when, it has been alleged, his position as a journalist in Athens was actually a cover for his ongoing work for British intelligence. In this period, he played a part in shaping modern Greece, be that for better or worse, and is still widely remembered in that country.

His untimely death means that the full story of Frank Macaskie's career may perhaps never be known, but enough pieces remain for us to conclude that he was an extraordinary man.

Chapter One

A Young Man Who Would Fight

Francis Gilbert Macaskie was born on 28 March 1912, the son of Thomas Septimus Macaskie (an advertising agent) and his wife Annie. At the time, the family lived at 10 Ingledew Crescent, Roundhay, Leeds, one of a row of smart houses built from Yorkshire stone, a few minutes' walk from Roundhay Park. The family already had one son, John Arthur Macaskie, who was three years older than Gilbert, as the boy was to be known by the family throughout his life, and four sisters would follow. The wider Macaskie clan were comfortably off, as evidenced by the fact that when his father's brother Francis Cunningham Macaskie died, he left a large and valuable estate, which an earlier divorce (unusual and somewhat scandalous before the First World War) had not managed to seriously deplete. The family originated in Montrose, Scotland where Francis senior had once been manager of the *Montrose Standard*. Gilbert's uncle had come to Leeds in 1881 as the result of negotiations with Lord Allerton to take over the *Leeds Daily News*. Francis Cunningham Macaskie had great ambitions for this small provincial newspaper, and in 1890 a Limited Liability Company had been formed. He retained the position of chairman of the directors, of what eventually became the *Yorkshire Evening News*. His brother Thomas had also become a director of the company, and by the 1930s his family were living at Primrose

Ville, Horsforth. Gilbert began his education at Moorlands School, Headingley, the oldest Prep School in Leeds, founded in 1897. In 1922 when Gilbert would have been there, it was a school of some seventy boys, who were being prepared for public school. The headmaster at this time was Mr J.H. Rawndrup and in an interview with the *Yorkshire Post* he described his, at the time, progressive views on aspects of education:

> I am a great believer in script writing. It is almost as quick, infinitely neater and makes spelling easier … we teach writing right through the school, though the fifth and sixth forms, ages about 12 to 14, have their teaching indirectly. They are allowed, as a privilege, to write in whichever style they prefer.[1]

From Moorlands, Macaskie attended the fee-paying Warwick School, and was Head of House and later Head of School from 1928 to 1931. He excelled both at sports and in other areas, indeed his litany of achievements is astounding, including on the cricket field, where he won the Lyttelton cup for batting, the Wood cup for bowling, and the Liddell cup for fielding. He was also awarded the Mercer cup for open fives, the Lakin bowl for the best shot, the bronze medallion for life saving, the Way prize for Divinity and the Sir William Collins cup for debating. His headmaster here, George A. Riding, later remembered:

> His quiet, winning personality brought it about that he was able to handle the school with never even a lifted voice, for every member of the school worshipped 'Mac.'

> He was captain of all the games that there were, but he had too a roving and active mind.[2]

George Riding – unwittingly, perhaps – had stirred up a huge controversy when remarks he made at a meeting of the Church of England Men's Society, late in 1930, were widely interpreted as an accusation that padres in the First World War were guilty of cowardice. He rather lamely tried to justify his comments afterwards by stating that he did not know that a reporter would be present, but the result was that columns of furious letters appeared in the local press just before Christmas that year. An even more controversial step, as it was to turn out, was his decision to marry Aideen Rolleston, daughter of T.W. Rolleston, the Irish author, and granddaughter of Stopford A. Brooke, poet and literary critic. Aideen was considerably younger than her husband, but the headmaster seemed to be unaware of the effect that she had on the teenage boys under his charge. As their son Christopher related in 2003:

> Several old Warwick boys commented to my father in later years that they didn't at all mind being caned by him because the chair over which they were asked to bend was positioned in such a way that, as they received their punishment, they were able to study his photograph of my mother who was, after all, only a few years older than themselves as well as being extremely good-looking![3]

Apart from her duties in the boarding house, Aideen Riding became much more involved in school life in December 1929 when, aged 25, she acted in a school play, Shakespeare's *Twelfth Night*, having stepped in to replace a boy who was ill. Officially-sanctioned females were in very short supply of course, in the all-male environment of a public school, and boys often took on women's roles, as in Shakespeare's own time. This performance must have been one of the first at Warwick School to have a real woman playing a female role, but, sadly, no photographs of this production seem to have survived. The 17-year-old who played Sebastian opposite Mrs Riding's Viola was Head Boy Frank Macaskie (as he was to be known throughout his life). Aideen must have made quite an impression on him, for he went as far as publishing a love poem to her in the December 1929 edition of the school magazine, *The Portcullis*. He did not put his name to it at the time, only admitting to his authorship several years later. It is not clear when the headmaster realised the nature of the poem, but by 1932 he was insisting that *The Portcullis* should have a permanent editor who was a member of staff, an arrangement which persists to the present day.

Macaskie went on to be Senior Prefect in his school house, Captain of the 1st XV and Captain of the 1st XI, and left the school in the summer of 1931. It has been claimed by some that Macaskie's relationship with Mrs Riding was more than just a schoolboy crush, but, as Christopher Riding has pointed out, Macaskie remained on friendly terms with both of his parents until he died, which makes the veracity of the claim seem unlikely.

The years after leaving school were difficult ones for Macaskie. Even his old headmaster admitted that for a time he appeared to be floundering. He worked at various jobs including as an assistant in a London department store. Eventually Riding managed to use his influence to get Macaskie a place at his *alma mater*, New College Oxford, to read law, and though he represented the university at fives, and had trials for both the golf and rugby teams, he left without completing his degree. He was back in Leeds around 1933 and 1934, but later took a role as an assistant golf professional alongside Tom Fernie at Royal Lytham & St Annes. Fernie had won the Scottish Professional Championship four times, in 1909, 1910, 1919 and 1920 and was runner-up in 1922 and 1925. He was also runner-up in the 1910 Dunlop Cup. In 1911 Fernie became club professional at Turnberry, and moved to Lytham in 1926. Golf had always been a big part of Macaskie's life, and at home he had won for his club, Horsforth, the Leeds and District four ball tournament, with his partner C.E. Richardson. The history of Royal Lytham & St Anne's Golf Club records that:

> A youngster called Frank Macaskie wrote to Fernie to ask him if he would take him as a premium apprentice. Tom already had two apprentices, one of whom was a Jewish refugee from Hitler's Germany. He was going to turn him down, but Macauley [his assistant] suggested that he should take him as the premium was £100 p.a. and worth having. Macaskie had been a law student at Cambridge University [sic] when his father, a news editor with the *Leeds Evening News*, died suddenly, leaving no money, and he could not continue his studies. When he came to Lytham, he was an 8 handicap golfer with a good swing but poor balance. Within six months this was put right

> and he entered the Fylde and North West Championship, winning it by ten shots against players of the calibre of Dick Burton and Phil Rodgers. Later he led the qualifiers in the *Leeds Evening News* Tournament and reached the semi-finals of the match play stage before he was beaten by Alf Padgham. Unfortunately he was seeing far too much of the wife of a Member and on refusing to break the liaison, he was sacked.[4]

It seems likely that the death of his uncle in 1933 was the real reason for Frank leaving his studies, because in fact it was he who had been paying his fees. After leaving Lytham, he took up a post in administration with Lancashire County Council in their offices at Preston. The 1939 Register, compiled in September of that year upon the outbreak of war, found Macaskie at a Lancaster guesthouse, though a newspaper report from twelve months earlier suggests he was actually living at Station Road, in the small Lancashire village of Hest Bank. His occupation in the Register was recorded as 'Secretary and Law Student,' indicating that he perhaps hoped to return to his studies at some point. An additional column shows that he was a member of the Officer Cadet Reserve and also registered for officer cadet training. Since the Munich Crisis of 1938, when war with Nazi Germany had finally appeared inevitable, Britain had been rapidly re-arming. However the country had a great deal of catching up to do if it was to reverse the reduction which had taken place in its military capability in the previous two decades. This decline was not restricted purely to materiel. In the eyes of many, it also extended to the moral fabric of the nation. In 1933, the Oxford Union, in a highly contentious debate, had resolved that under no circumstances would its members fight for King and Country. The vote caused dismay among the older generation, not least because it offered encouragement to the dictatorships now growing in strength across the Channel. Frank Macaskie proved that not every young man of his generation and social background supported this viewpoint.

The clouds of war had not merely gathered, by now it was fair to say that the sky had taken on a distinctly ominous hue. British troops were entrenched in France, busily but wrongheadedly preparing to fight the previous war (in some cases even taking over the same positions). Meanwhile Poland, which Britain had pledged to support, was in the final stages of being dismembered by the Nazis and Soviets. British troops would soon be driven out of France and Belgium in the humiliating debacle leading up to Dunkirk, but a consequence of this would be that for the next eighteen months the pendulum of war for the British Empire would swing away from Europe, towards the cauldron of North Africa and the Middle East. Macaskie, though he could not know this yet, was to be in the vanguard of the action there.

Chapter Two

A New Diomedes

Frank Macaskie was called up for war service on 9 March 1940 and was posted initially to the depot of the Leicestershire Regiment at Glen Parva Barracks, near Wigston. We know that he was there in April 1940, as he represented the regiment at the funeral of the Duke of Rutland at Belvoir Castle. Before long however he was posted to the 1st/5th Battalion of the Leicesters. This Territorial Army formation had just received a severe mauling in the Norway campaign, for which it was ill-prepared and ill-equipped. It was now in Scotland, rebuilding, and receiving reinforcements to replace those officers and men who had either been captured by the Germans, or interned in neutral Sweden. However, it would never see active service again, instead, later in the war becoming an officer training battalion. After returning from Norway (where its commanding officer Guy German had been captured) it was taken over by Lieutenant Colonel Colin Callander, who, the regimental history admits, was faced with a difficult task, but not long afterwards the battalion settled down to the job of rebuilding. Shortly after Macaskie joined, the unit moved to Caledon, and later Carrickfergus, in Northern Ireland. Much of the time here was spent setting up road blocks, and working closely with the local Home Guard. The security situation in this part of the United Kingdom was a perilous one. The Atlantic coast of Ireland was particularly vulnerable to incursions by the Germans, and the low level campaign, which had been conducted by the IRA since the partition of Ireland in 1922, was not suspended during the war. One of the highlights of his sojourn with the 1st/5th battalion would have been an inspection visit in July by Anthony Eden, then Secretary of State for War. Macaskie was in C Company, and this formation was selected to demonstrate 'Company in Attack' for the Minister. However in November 1940 the *Green Tiger*, regimental magazine of the Leicestershire Regiment, reported that: 'The Company has had a few changes in officers and men. We were extremely unfortunate in losing Lieutenant Macaskie, who has gone to warmer climes, and we wish him good luck in his new post.'[1]

Macaskie's new posting was ultimately to the 2nd Battalion of the Leicestershire Regiment, which was at that time in Egypt, as part of the 16th Infantry Brigade. The journey to join them however was a long and monotonous one; with the Mediterranean at this point in the war effectively an Italian lake, the troopship, from the Canadian Pacific Steamship Company took the long route down the west coast of Africa and round the Cape of Good Hope. For the officers, the monotony was broken only by endless games of Bridge. There was ready access to alcohol in the ship's saloon, and 'Rye and Dry' (Rye whisky and dry ginger) was a popular drink among the officers. At the end of November they finally went ashore, and travelled by Egyptian State Railways to the Infantry Base Depot at Geneifa, a tented camp where reinforcements and returning wounded waited to be posted to an active service unit.

Here, messing for officers was charged at 4/- a day, which was considered far too expensive, and was generally grumbled at, but the food was very good, and plentiful, with any amount of fresh fruit and vegetables available. The flies were a dreadful nuisance and as this was winter, it could only be imagined what they must be like in the summer. They crawled on all surfaces and on food if allowed to. The weather however was glorious. The sun shone brilliantly from six in the morning, until five in the evening, when it disappeared, abruptly, but not before producing a wonderful sunset. It was very warm during the day, and the general dress was an open shirt and shorts – except when the wind blew and then a jersey was necessary as well. It was most unpleasant when the wind did blow, as the sand came up with it, and got into eyes, mouth and hair, filling the ears and also into the food. Clothes, bedding and everything in the tents were also covered. It gave some idea of what a sandstorm in the desert must be like. The evenings and nights were fairly cold – most officers wore their cotton drill suits at this time. There was little to do here to fill an officer's leisure time. There was some pleasant bathing which was indulged in by many. There was also an open air cinema, but being open air the acoustics were poor, and therefore the sound was not good.

A few days after their arrival, Macaskie and two officers with whom he had become friends on the journey named Harry Massey and Rex Rangecroft applied for and obtained leave, and decided to make the journey to Cairo. Massey's letters home provide an insight into how they spent the four days. They arrived up there very late on Wednesday night, and stayed at the Continental Hotel: this was an enormous establishment and really a very pleasant one; it was the second-best hotel in the city – the best, Shepheards being closed, until 1 December. They had special prices for the army, and as the group only paid 6/- for bed & breakfast, this seemed at first rather reasonable. However it had a sting in its tail, because drinks and meals were at the very best London prices, so the establishment intended to get its money back that way. The three officers ate and drank elsewhere, so overall the cost worked out quite well.

On the Friday, it was a hot and beautiful day and so they went out to the Gezira Sporting Club, which is about two miles outside the city. This was a wonderful place, and contained a race course, an 18-hole golf course, tennis courts, squash courts, fives courts, a large swimming pool, a billiard room, an enormous bar and restaurant both inside and outside. It cost them 3/- for the day, and this included everything except food and drink. Frank and Harry had a round of golf in the morning and both played quite well despite using borrowed clubs. Then they had a pleasant omelette and salad lunch, followed by a bask in the sun, and then a bathe. Drinks were very cheap here, and in the evening they met a variety of people, and drank so much and for so long, that they missed dinner altogether, and eventually stumbled back to the hotel and went to bed.

The Sunday was the day arranged for a journey to Memphis and historic sites. They were up early and met Abdul, the guide, and the taxi, just before 9am. Their first destination was Memphis, this being a little over one hour's drive from Cairo, and all the way travelling along the banks of the Nile. They then went to Sakhara, which was in the desert and not so very far away. Here they were set on by a horde of locals wanting to sell post cards, scarabs, and other souvenirs, as well as take them to the tombs on donkeys – but they ignored all these. After this, they had lunch at Mena, which is within half a mile of the Pyramids of Gizeh and the Sphinx, and then went to have a look at these. They then drove back to Cairo, and through the old town, to the Blue Mosque. This they found was a complete disappointment. They went through the requirement of taking their shoes off, putting on some obviously well-worn and dirty looking slippers, but found the inside consisted of some rather plain walls, a pair of poor looking minarets and no roof. Interestingly, whilst they were out at the Pyramid and Sphinx, they had their fortunes told by an old man – one of those sitting in the sand. He told Frank that he was loved by several, but that the only one who mattered was not his wife.

Previously, on the troopship journey Macaskie had confided in his close friend Massey that he had no intention whatsoever may happen, and however long he may be away, of being unfaithful in even the smallest way to the woman he loved. At that point he was 28, and had been in love with her for seven years. She was aged 36 at least, and had two boys, one aged 16 and the other 14, both at Malvern College; she had a husband who was in business in Manchester, and very wealthy, and who thought of nothing but business. Macaskie could only sleep with her when the husband was away on business in America, which happened fairly often. She did not sleep with her husband, and he knew all about the affair. It was only the two sons which kept them together.

On the night that he was due to leave Britain for active service, Macaskie had been so heartbroken he could hardly speak. A letter from Massey to his wife, dated 30 January 1941, reads:

> I had a letter from Frank Macaskie yesterday. You remember I told you he had come to see me off to Palestine – apparently he arrived back at the I.B.D in the early hours of the morning, & a complete daze, & was woken up shortly afterwards, & told that he was off to the Western Desert. It seems he very nearly missed the train. He says he is now living in an Italian dug-out, & being bitten to bits by fleas. He had a letter from his Mary, the very day he left - & has had two more since. He says they were a great relief & joy to him, but made him acutely & almost unbearably aware of how unhappy he is. That is what I like about Frank & why we get on so well together. He is such a grand fellow – & yet he is just as miserable as I am – & so we never had any false notions or expectations about enjoying ourselves, & never made the mistake of trying to do so. It saves so much trouble - & money too.[2]

Macaskie had been urgently drafted to the 2nd Battalion Leicestershire Regiment, which had just received its first major taste of action at Sidi Barani in December 1940. This battle, which has now become something of a lost footnote in history, was actually remarkably important at the time. Whilst not being a turning point in the war, it was still significant as Britain's first victory against Axis forces. Italian troops had been decisively trounced, though the Leicesters had suffered some casualties, hence the sudden need for reinforcements.

The battalion, one of two Regular Army formations in the regiment, had been in the Middle East for some time, having been involved in suppressing the Arab Revolt in Palestine. In September 1940, it moved by train to the Western Desert, the brigade now coming under the command of the 4th Indian Division, in order to counter the threat posed by Italian forces in Libya. Italy's entry into the war in June 1940 brought a new theatre of operations into being, along the border between its own territory and that of Egypt, a British protectorate. Mussolini, eager to impress his ally Hitler, had boasted that he would sweep the British out of Egypt and seize the vitally important Suez Canal. If Britain lost control of this waterway, the most direct route to India, then her empire would be cut in half.

The only force standing in his way was 'Wavell's 30,000', the force commanded by Sir Archibald Wavell, consisting of Britons, Australians, New Zealanders, South Africans and Indians. Wavell knew that he was massively outnumbered by the Italians, and that if they launched an attack they would be difficult to stop. His initial plan was just to hold them up, until reinforcements could arrive. His opponent was Italian General Graziani; after some initial skirmishing in the desert, Graziani made his move in September, and the British fell back to their prepared base at Mersa Matruh. The Italians themselves found difficulties of supply and reinforcement in the desert, and Graziani halted to dig in at Sidi Barani. In total secrecy the British moved troops up and launched their counter attack. The Italian defensive perimeter was too long and too weakly defended, and the British including 2nd Leicesters were able to punch through, taking some 38,000 prisoners along with numerous tanks, trucks and guns.

Between 13 and 19 December the battalion moved first to Buq Buq, then to Wadi Shaba, near Halfaya Pass. At Buq Buq they were employed on water point duties at the wells and on guarding and evacuating prisoners. The desert fleas were now their constant companions in these captured positions and the only relief from them came from the occasional bathe in the sea, which was enjoyable despite the cold. Wadi Shaba was, like all wadis, dry except on one or two days of the year. It had been used by the Italians as a bivouac area, and was soon christened 'Flea Wadi' by all. Every crevice seemed to swarm with the hungry brutes. From here the 2nd Leicesters were kept busy in unloading stores and petrol arriving in Salum Harbour for the two armoured brigades which were now leading the advance. This task was far from being a pleasant one, as the port was frequently bombed, or shelled by a long-range gun nicknamed 'Bardia Bill.' On 19 December the battalion relieved the 2nd Rifle Brigade in front of Bardia, and it was an eerie journey by lorry in the moonlight up the winding road which climbed from Salum Harbour up to the escarpment above. The relief was completed by 1am – a bitterly cold wind was blowing across the top of the escarpment and so the battalion took shelter in the tops of the wadis which ran down to the sea. Here it was too rocky to dig in, and defences were created by building up stone sangars. Activity here was confined to carrier patrols by day, and foot patrols by night. On at least one occasion the latter were fired upon by Italians dug in in front of Bardia.

On 23 December the battalion went into Brigade reserve in the Wadi Aqrab area. Christmas was spent here, the Padre visiting the company areas, and festive spirit being enhanced by the arrival of Second-in-Command Major Phillips from Alexandria with beer and chocolate for all, a welcome addition to the usual salty water, bully beef and biscuits. They moved back in lorries to Buq Buq once more, in time for New Year's Eve, the festivities being enlivened by some captured Italian cognac. On 2 January however the battalion was suddenly recalled to Bardia to be in reserve for the assault carried out by the 6th Australian Division the next day. They moved by route march, covering fifteen miles the first day and eight the second. The battalion was now called forward and dispersed on different duties. D Company was on the water point at Fort Gapuzzo. A Company was running a PoW cage on the frontier fence nearby, and the remainder were either escorting prisoners or salvaging enemy equipment. In forty-eight hours the number of prisoners held by the battalion rose from 3,000 to 10,000, and with the limited food and water available, provisioning this number was quite a challenge. It was only met by distributing captured enemy rations, before the prisoners were escorted to ships at Salum harbour. In the end some 33,000 Italians had passed through their hands.

Tobruk also fell to Australian troops on 22 January, and once again the battalion was called forward for PoW escort duties in the wake of the battle. This was a major achievement, for Tobruk was the only deepwater port in North Africa.

Whoever controlled it, controlled the main port of supply for fuel and other essentials. By now, the battalion were settled at Wadi Homer, where salvaging and mine clearance continued. Training also started in earnest for new NCOs and signallers, and the numerous reinforcements recently received. On 29 January they received their first issue of serge battledress, which was welcome and long overdue, the khaki cotton drill in which they were currently equipped being inadequate for the bitterly cold nights. In February Cairo leave commenced once more, and parties left the battalion throughout the month. On 13 February the battalion arrived at Tahag Camp, situated on flat barren earth some fifteen miles north of Ismailia. Given the circumstances it was pleasant enough, with no fleas to contend with, and hot showers available. On 22 February the battalion celebrated a belated Christmas, Major Phillips again coming to the fore with an excellent dinner of turkey and Christmas pudding arranged. In spite of this diversion however there was still much training and reorganisation to be done. On top of this, the battalion was suddenly put onto combined operations training. After studying the theory, it moved at the end of March to Kabrit and bivouacked to take part in practical training as an assault landing force, the intention being to effect some sort of landing on Rhodes. However, the training was abruptly halted (and the plan abandoned) amid rumours of misfortunes in the desert.

On 5 April the battalion was ordered to hand over some vehicles to the 22nd Guards Brigade which were hurrying to the scene, and on 9 April the Leicesters themselves entrained at Geneifa, bound for Mersa Matruh and the desert once more.

On arrival they took over the east sector from the Coldstream Guards, and the first task was the rather disheartening one of digging out the defences constructed the previous year, which had been completely filled with sand in the many desert storms which had blown up since. Moreover, their old friends the fleas were present in force, and seemed hungrier than ever. Rumours and counter-rumours filtered back with units that came down from the front line, but when D company were sent to Sidi Barani for four days to work at the dumps they came back with the heartening news that the Australians were still holding out gallantly at Tobruk. Later in April the battalion was relieved by 23rd Australian Brigade, and returned to their old positions in the Baggush Box, which again had to be dug out as they had filled with sand.

The commanding officer of the 2nd Leicesters at this time was Lieutenant Colonel C.H.V. Cox MC. Still a bachelor at 40, Cox had been awarded his MC during the First World War. He had served with the 1st Battalion in India for many years between the wars and was on his way home to England via Egypt when he was asked to take over command of the 2nd Battalion. He had a regular soldier's eye for detail, and was a strict disciplinarian. His coolness under fire was legendary, and he inspired confidence in those around him. In action he was quick to assess a situation and act accordingly. The other officers in the battalion were a mix of pre-war Regular Army (such as the Adjutant, Captain J.H. Marriott, and company commanders including Major G.G.B. Anderson and Captain A.W.D. Nicholls) and temporary officers, many of whom had come to it via the Middle East OCTU in Cairo. Yet one of the most remarkable features about this unit was the camaraderie between officers of all types and ages, and between the officers and other ranks as well. It was certainly thought to be better than that in other units with which the 2nd Leicesters came into contact. In April 1941, Massey received news from Macaskie, which he relayed to his wife. His words were prescient:

> I had quite a long letter from Frank Macaskie the other day, which I was very glad to have. He congratulated me on being about to be a major, & said 'I know you will rise even higher than that, for I know of no one more capable of holding any rank that may be open to you'! Which I thought was extremely civil of him, & quite heartening, coming from Frank. He went on to say that he was in the ghastly position of being unable to rise, except into dead men's shoes. It is bad luck, really, I certainly know of no better officer than Frank. He had had another five days leave in Cairo – and had tried to get up to Palestine, but had not been allowed. He said he had spent all the time with Gerald Ecclestone [a friend from the I.B.D.] – the day time at Gezira – & the evenings at various cabarets – Gerald to dance & Frank to drink. But that at midnight their ways parted – Frank's to his own bed – and Gerald's to some woman's. I do hope Frank gets through alright – it seems his battalion is in a pretty crack Division.[3]

Frank and his comrades would not know it yet, but events now were moving fast on the other side of the Mediterranean. Few campaigns in the Second World War have as much drama or capture the imagination in the same way as does the battle for Crete in May 1941. Put simply, both sides recognised the island's key position in the Aegean, and both sides meant to have it. Following Italy's unsuccessful invasion of Greece via Albania, in April 1941 Germany entered the fray by attacking on a new front. Prime Minister Winston Churchill had committed forces that Britain could ill-afford to spare from the desert war to the gallant assistance of the Greek army. When these men were driven out by the lightning Axis drive through Bulgaria and on towards Athens, Crete became their refuge, and Churchill formulated a plan to turn the island into another Malta, a bastion which would halt the German advance in the eastern Mediterranean. Hitler meanwhile saw it as the springboard for his next offensive, and agreed to the paratrooper commander General Kurt Student's plan to take it, using the biggest airborne assault in history. Five thousand elite *Fallschirmjaeger* would land on the island, aiming to capture its three airfields and other key points. The ensuing battle was to be a ferocious one, and the 2nd Battalion Leicestershire Regiment would be in the thick of it.

After months of hard weary toil in the desert, on 12 May 1941 their brigade commander had declared a general holiday for troops under his command. Many of the members of the 2nd Leicesters were enjoying a well-earned rest on the Mediterranean coast the following day, when suddenly orders to pack up and leave were received. Trucks and stores were handed over to neighbouring formations, and the battalion entrained late that night bound for Alexandria docks and an unknown destination. So hurried was the move in fact that some officers and men on leave in Cairo or on courses could not be recalled in time, and after loading stores and equipment into two Royal Navy cruisers, HMS *Fiji* and HMS *Gloucester*, the battalion set sail without them. There had not even been time to complete a proper muster list for the battalion. Everyone who embarked was simply asked to write his name and number on a piece of paper. The pieces were collected together in an envelope and handed to a bemused embarkation officer on the dockside.

Their destination however was now becoming clear. They were going to Crete. Those in a position to know were also aware that the battalion was about to become a mobile reserve for the 14th Infantry Brigade, defending Heraklion and its airfield. The crossing was rough, and most of the battalion were glad when the cruisers reached the Cretan capital around midnight on 15 May. The pressure to unload the ships quickly was intense, as in daylight hours the docks were regularly subjected to enemy air attacks. Indeed, no sooner had the battalion proceeded inland, dumped their equipment in their new positions, and began brewing tea, than first light brought with it a raid by enemy Messerschmitts machine gunning targets below. Battalion cook Private John Lippett, attached from the Army Catering Corps, was busy preparing breakfast for the men when the raid scattered the kitchen staff and sent the cutlery and pans flying in all directions. Air attack was a new experience for the battalion, as by and large the Italian *Regia Aeronautica* had not been a problem in the desert campaign, but this was to set the pattern for the coming week.

With the raid over, the men had an opportunity to examine their new surroundings. Instead of the featureless expanses of the Western Desert they found themselves looking across a landscape of hills covered with vineyards and olive groves; of fields of wheat swaying gently in the breeze and small settlements of whitewashed houses. The battalion was dispersed around Heraklion, and the various companies set about digging themselves in under the shelter of the numerous olive trees. Following the withdrawal from Greece, the defence of Crete was entrusted to Major General Bernard Freyberg VC, commander of the New Zealand Division and hero of the First World War. Freyberg however was convinced that any German assault would come from the sea, and neglected to plan for an air attack, despite intelligence suggesting that this was from where it would come. Once the battle was underway, communication between Allied formations was poor, and Freyberg would fail to move them quickly enough to trouble spots, with some units sitting idly as others fought against overwhelming odds.

The morning of 20 May 1941 started off quietly enough, but it was to be a day like no other that the battalion had experienced. In the early part of the afternoon things were so peaceful that the commanding officer was having a bath, in the last remaining hotel that was so equipped. However, at 3.45 pm news came through that Australian troops were entertaining paratroopers at Chania, to the west. A motorcyclist sent to fetch the CO from his bath was machined gunned by a low flying Messerschmitt, and the sky was now filled with hostile planes. The battalion was subjected to an intense air attack, but by 5.20 pm this was dying away, and when looking out to sea, men observed a series of twinkling flashes of light, like stars. This turned out to be the sun reflecting on the glass of an armada of Junkers Ju 52 troop carrying aircraft. As they turned into their drop formation, the air was filled with parachutes, many of brilliant colours. Flying in V configuration, the two outer aircraft of each section dropped paratroopers, whilst the central aircraft dropped supplies, as indicated by the coloured chutes. Two aircraft were shot down by the battalion Anti-Aircraft machine guns, others were claimed by nearby Bofors guns. As the parachutists descended, many were killed or wounded. Corporal Tom Marston, of Battalion Headquarters remembered:

> Down came these aeroplanes, flying really low, it was awe inspiring … and then somebody said, "F…ing Hell," he said, "Look here," and out piles these sticks of paras, well we were there, and we each had fifty rounds, and they came down so slowly, and of those sticks that came down [near us] nobody lived. Definitely not. I mean, we couldn't miss them. They came down say about 300 yards away, and every one was shot, in the air as they came down or just as they landed. They never got up to sort themselves out. That was a bit of free shooting, but after that we were collared and organised.[4]

Drop zones where the enemy had succeeded in landing were identified, and companies told off to deal with them. By 6.15pm, Macaskie's C Company had gone, as the regimental history puts it, 'like hounds unleashed' under their commander Captain Donald S. Carden to the area known as Buttercup

Field, near Poros. Here the company found itself fighting alongside two companies of the Australian 2/4th Battalion, which had latterly come out of the debacle in Greece. They had left behind most of their equipment, so the Leicesters lent them two of their six mortars and crews. At the end of the day, orders were issued for all companies to return within the perimeter, except for C Company which could not be located. They did not return until the following morning. The task for the following day would seem to be the rapid liquidation of the two remaining pockets of resistance – within Heraklion town and east of the aerodrome. The battalion War Diary estimated that in the immediate vicinity some 2,000 paratroopers had landed, and that more than one third of these had been killed or wounded.

The following day, 21 May, was by comparison fairly quiet. C Company returned at about 0700 and went into reserve. Pockets of the enemy within the battalion perimeter were duly mopped up. The battalion was however sniped and mortared by German troops outside the perimeter. Throughout the day Messerschmitts made low flying attacks to try to erode morale, but the battalion held its ground, and the enemy was actually driven from the town, and no hostile reinforcements were observed. Early the following morning the battalion moved forward again, searching the immediate area for arms, ammunition and casualties. During the day another large-scale assault appeared to develop, with supplies being dropped to the east of the aerodrome. C Company moved to join B Company in readiness for an attack on enemy positions the next day. Early on 23 May, B and C Companies were sent to assist the

Black Watch (the Royal Highland Regiment) in clearing the enemy from the eastern side of the airfield. Here they became caught up in a terrific fire-fight. Private Stan Seddon of the Leicesters, a member of C Company, takes up the story:

> We started off as it got dusk, and we went through the Black Watch lines, and at dawn we went down a gully and came up a steepish hill, and when we got to the brim there was a space of what, 300 yards, and there were rocks all over, but there was one row of rocks on the edge of the airfield. I suppose when they had cleared the airfield they'd just shovelled them out of the way, but [the Germans] were using them as a defensive position. We didn't know. Of course they were waiting for us. How they got to know about us, I don't know, but then we went in. C Company went in, there was [Macaskie's] 13 Platoon, 14 Platoon and 15 Platoon. I was in 15 Platoon ... well it were a shambles. Half way across this 300 yard stretch they opened up with everything they'd got, and they'd quite a bit, and we couldn't do nothing. They were entrenched at the back of these rocks, blokes got mowed down, and we took shelter at the back of some rocks. I was not far from the officer, and he'd been shot through the leg, another lad from the Halifax draft, Jack Saunders, he'd been shot through the leg, so they couldn't move. He was yelling, was the officer, "We've walked into a trap," he says, "who can get out, get out. Save yourselves, you'll be able to fight again." There was a lull in the firing, whether they were running out of

> ammunition, I don't know, but I think they were getting ready for a bayonet charge. They'd seen how many had come, and of course them who could move, had to get up and go, and we did go, and when we got to the end of this rocky field, where it dipped down we were alright, but we had to keep going to this ridge to be really safe, because they wouldn't show themselves in the open.[5]

It remains a possibility that that the officer who was shouting was actually Macaskie, though two other battalion officers had also been wounded and left behind in this incident, Second Lieutenant H.E.G. Collett and Second Lieutenant A.R. Markham. Private Jack Saunders, for his part, remembered that, despite his injury, he was still able to tend to those in a more serious condition:

> It wasn't a serious wound. It was only a flesh wound, but it did lose a lot of blood, and other colleagues weren't so fortunate. And I went to the aid of one young chap who had been shot and the order to withdraw was given, but by that time we were really tied down by rifle fire, machine gun fire and I helped this other chap and he was obviously dying, and I stayed with him, and I was actually taken prisoner that same evening.[6]

He remembered later that he was initially unconcerned about being captured, believing that as the British still controlled most of the island, it was only a temporary situation and he would soon be rejoining his battalion. His wound was treated by the Germans, and the following morning the prisoners were actually bombed by a British plane; the fight to keep the airfield out of German hands however was lost, and the consequence of this, together with the capture by the Germans of the airfield at Maleme, was that they could now pour troops into Crete at will. Freyberg's defence of the island, and the mistakes that he had made in the course of it, had underlined the fact that his unquestionable personal bravery at junior level did not automatically translate into effective leadership, of the kind that was necessary to fight a modern, fast-moving battle such as this.

In the fighting at the airfield Macaskie had been shot three times. One of the bullets had passed through his abdomen and had missed his spine by just half an inch. Others hit his arm and leg. He was left, in agony, under a bridge, with the German wounded. After his own men had withdrawn, he too was given medical treatment by the Germans, and then like Saunders he was loaded along with the German casualties from the action onto a Junkers Ju52 transport plane. He was flown out of Crete to Athens, where he was treated at a PoW hospital. After recovery from his wounds, he recuperated at a nearby makeshift camp. From the description that we have it is not clear where in today's Nikaia the wartime temporary prisoner camp was located. Since it was near a hospital, which presumably was an existing facility that had been requisitioned, it would probably have been near the so-called 'General Hospital of Piraeus', which is still functioning in a much renovated and extended form in more or less the same place that it was then. As for the prisoner camp, the only thing that we can tell from the scant descriptions that we have is that it consisted of barracks surrounded by open space and enclosed by a barbed wire fence, itself separated by a road from houses where the Greek people lived. All these disappeared a long time ago, since Kokkinia-Nikaia is now a densely built-up satellite municipality of Piraeus. Both hospital and prisoner camp were working at full capacity in late May and early June 1941, when the Battle of Crete was in its last phases before its official end on 1 June.

From there Macaskie escaped along with four companions – three other officers and a pipe major of the Black Watch – with the help of the legendary resistance leader Lela Karagianni and her people – among them the brothers Elias and Sotirios Papavassiliou, bakers, who had an oven opposite the hospital. The fugitives fled to the mountains, in the region of St George's Bay but one of the officers was still suffering badly from a wound to the head, and they were forced to seek help in a Greek village, even though they half-thought it would lead to recapture. As it turned out, the villagers could not do enough for them, and brought the fugitives into their homes to care for them. Even though food was beginning to get scarce in Greece at this point, they fed the British prisoners from their own meagre rations. This kindness from ordinary Greek people made a deep impression on Macaskie, and from here sprang his love of Greece. Days went by, and there was no prospect of help, but one of the villagers knew a man in Athens named Georgios Trypanis, who spoke English, and might be able to help. In September 1941, Trypanis would organise Macaskie's escape from Keratea bound for Samos, with a boat that could take him and his four companions. From there they were processed in Cesme, where they were taken in by British consul Noël Rees, of whom more later. The next stage of Macaskie's military career was about to begin. It was one which would see him leave behind the 'conventional' role that he had previously undertaken as an infantry platoon commander, and move into much more dangerous, clandestine territory.

Chapter Three

Greek Adventures

With the end of the Crete debacle, the survivors of the 2nd Leicesters were evacuated from the island by the Royal Navy, while under assault from relentless air attack. Though it is not in the nature of soldiers to praise the navy, all agreed that the skill and heroism shown by the senior service in avoiding German bombing was outstanding. The campaign however was regarded as a defeat, and despite the bravery shown in battle, decorations were as a result sparsely awarded. Whilst Macaskie was recuperating in a German hospital, it took some time for details of his fate – and whereabouts – to be communicated via the Red Cross. In the immediate aftermath of the fighting on Crete it appears that Frank was believed to have been killed. A letter from his friend, Harry Massey of the East Kent Regiment to his wife reveals:

> I'm afraid that Frank Macaskie is dead, killed in action in Crete. It's a tragedy isn't it? I'm afraid it must be true. Among the various things of which I am in charge here is the Detention Barracks & I heard yesterday that there were 3 soldiers from the Leicesters there. So I sent word to the Police NCO to ask them if they knew anything about Frank & they told him this. He asked them were they sure because it was the Major who was enquiring

into a great friend of his & they said there was no doubt they knew him well & had all liked him & thought what a fine chap he was. I feel a tremendous loss here my darling I think I must have conveyed to you in my letters how very fond of him I was & quite apart from perhaps meeting him for leave out here I was looking forward to having him as one of our very best friends after the war at home.

There is no doubt at all that you would have liked him tremendously & that the three of us & I expect his poor unhappy girlfriend too would have had very much in common. On thinking of Frank the last few weeks & though I only knew him for 3½ months I feel certain that I liked him more than any man I have ever known including Vernon & Frank & Gordon & all of them. He was very good fun & as you know we had some marvellous drinking parties together. But over & above that & so much more important of course he was such a fine chap – so very intelligent & sensible & so well read & educated & so very interesting to talk to & listen to. And he was so bloody pleasant & unselfish & so kindly & sympathetic & understanding. And yet very stern in his outlook & character in many ways. And dear old Frank he was so genuinely fond of me & interested in me & would have done anything for me. And he was looking forward, just as much as I was, to all the fun & interest we would all have together when we were home again. I feel dreadfully depressed & dejected & angry. He was

> such a dear fellow, old Frank & you know how difficult I find it to make friends & he was one in a million & quite irreplaceable.
>
> I got to know him slowly & as you know I preferred Rex for some time. But I don't really mind whether I see Rex again or not, but I shall remember & regret Frank for a very long time to come. I will tell you much more about him when I come home. And I will write his mother a long letter. I'm sure she will be pleased to hear from somebody who knew him well out here, who was so fond of him. Otherwise, she will only get a rather stereotyped sort of letter from his CO. You know it seems to me so utterly wrong that a man like Frank 28 years of age, a fine leader of men – he had a very good way with them & they liked & respected him – with a first class brain & obvious ability – should have to be a Second Lieutenant & a Platoon Commander easily the most consistently dangerous job in the Army. And yet bumped up brainless little idiots who have been a few years in the Regular or Territorial Army should command companies.[1]

A few days later, Macaskie's name was among those mentioned in a German radio broadcast as being a prisoner – the first intimation that his family would have that he was safe. During the weeks in which he was recuperating in the German hospital, it would appear that he was in correspondence with the Adjutant of the 2nd Leicesters, Captain John Marriott. Many years later Marriott recalled in a conversation with the author that the battalion were anxious to discover what had happened to Major G.G.B. Anderson of B Company. Badly wounded in the stomach in the battle at the aerodrome, he had known he was fatally injured and ordered his stretcher bearers to leave him. Since then, they had had no word of him, but in order to try to clarify matters Macaskie wrote to the German commander at Heraklion. This man it seems had been to the same English public school as Anderson, and this common ground was the basis of the request for information, but the Heraklion commander could offer nothing further.

Macaskie's first escape from German captivity was to result in the award of the Military Cross. The official recommendation, prepared by Brigadier J. Shearer, Director of Military Intelligence, records that after capture he and the two officers who were with him,

> Were transported by aeroplane to Athens a few days later and taken to the hospital at Nea Kokkinia where they remained about a month. From the hospital they were sent to a P/W convalescent camp in the same neighbourhood. They remained here only about a fortnight before they effected their escape about the middle of July. After his escape Lieutenant Macaskie remained in hiding in Athens and area for two months, during which time he was able to collect a great deal of valuable information and to make a large number of contacts with friendly civilians for future use. He made contact with persons aiding Imperial Service personnel to escape from Greece and was of considerable help to them.

> After his stay in Athens he arranged for himself and two other officers to be evacuated to British territory via Turkey. They travelled to a point on the coast east of Keratea. where they embarked as arranged on the 12th September 1941. With only one stop, at the island of Cyarus (Jura) [Gyaros] they arrived at Khushadasi [Kuşadası] in Turkey and thence were passed on to Cairo. On his arrival at GHQ Lieutenant Macaskie volunteered to return to Greece to organise and conduct the escape of further Imperial Service personnel, who he knew to be in hiding in Greece. His previous experience as an escaper and his great foresight in setting up for his return a number of contacts and friends in Athens made this project possible. This officer is now working in connection with the organisation and facilitation of the escape of Imperial service personnel, his work being co-ordinated with that of others and a number of successful escapes have been the result. These however would not have been possible but for the courage, resource, coolness and initiative of this officer. Thus this officer not only brought back valuable information and helped two officers to escape with him, but is still doing magnificent work behind the enemy lines where, thanks to his courage, daring and initiative he has made possible the escape of many of our men.[2]

The first escape must have been one of the easiest for Macaskie. Having made careful notes on the movements of the guards, he and his fellow escapers, Lieutenants Collett and

Markham from the Leicesters and the other two, identities now unknown, were able to cut their way through the barbed wire fence surrounding the camp. After being hidden and fed by local people from the Karagianni organisation in Athens they travelled, disguised as Greeks, to the hills before being placed under the protection of Georgios Trypanis, Cambridge graduate and former manager of the Athens electric tram system, which was subsequently run by a German philhellene and anti-Nazi, Edgar Thomashausen. Trypanis and his wife, Besy Adosidou, known for her Red Cross volunteer work on the Albanian front, were among the first, together with the engineer Konstantinos Katris, to create a team for the gathering of military personnel intelligence following the flight of the British from Athens. They operated as 'Mr and Mrs Baum.' There were many close calls for Macaskie during this period; one day whilst travelling in a tram carriage with Trypanis, it collided with a German staff car. The German driver boarded and began to take down the names of the occupants. Frank at this time could not speak a word of Greek, but as the German approached him Trypanis saved the situation, by saying that the tram driver was at fault and as manager he took full responsibility. The German went away satisfied. Macaskie first hid in the Trypanis house, then in the house of Ieta Xydi, on Ypsilantou Street. However, he was not the sort of man who could live locked up in an apartment. Recklessly, according to reports, he walked around Kolonaki and declared himself British to anyone who asked him. Finally, the fugitives were taken to the coast where they boarded a fishing boat bound for neutral Turkey. Having arrived here, they were not interned but passed straight into the hands of the British consul Noël Rees. He put them on a train to Aleppo, from which place they went by car to Damascus and then by train again to Jerusalem and on to Egypt, to reach the British military authorities in Cairo. On his way back, Frank made time to call on his old friend Massey:

> You could definitely have knocked me over with a feather & fanned my brow, when word came to me last Saturday that '2/Lt Macaskie' wanted to speak to me on the phone. I sprinted, & it really was Frank, from Jerusalem. He had been wounded, a bullet in the buttock, straight through, & out at the other side – taken prisoner by the Germans, & well looked after & doctored by them – then put in a prisoner of war camp. He decided very early on that this was no place for him & after many varied & exciting adventures, about which I may not tell you, he arrived in Palestine. Poor Frank – he has lost all his kit, every stitch & piece – all his photographs – & all his letters. I know exactly how he feels. And now, having been posted as dead, even in the English papers, he has to start all over again, getting his address straight, & waiting months until he is answering letters which are in reply to his letters.
>
> He was still in a peculiar set of borrowed civilian clothes – or at least, they had been presented to him by friendly natives. I met him in Tel Aviv – & we came back here & talked & talked. Sunday we just spent quietly, & I had

> work to do – & in the evening we made a pretty big hole in a bottle of whisky. On Monday I took him up to Jerusalem, where he had to report, & I had some things I had to do. And on Tuesday morning he went off to Cairo.[3]

Back at home, Macaskie's arrival was reported in the *Green Tiger* in an article penned by adjutant John Marriott: '2nd Lieutenants Macaskie, Collett and Markham, all wounded and presumed prisoners of war in Crete, have contrived to get back and report back for duty with wounds healed. A stout effort.'[4]

Privately, Macaskie confided in Marriott that one of the others had been less than keen to try to escape, and he had had a lot of trouble getting him to go. Although the *Green Tiger* would continue to offer snippets of information about him as it got them for the remainder of the war, this was in fact Macaskie's last direct association with the Leicestershire Regiment. Sources attest however to the fact that he remained proud of his involvement with it, for the rest of his life. Macaskie now came to the attention of British Intelligence in Cairo; with a steady flow of returning evaders from Greece it had become evident to members of 'A' Force, the escape and evasion arm of British Intelligence's MI9, that a number of official rescue missions should be launched to try to round up those men still on the run. MI9's operations in the Middle East were set up by Colonel Dudley Clarke, who had served under Wavell in Palestine before the war. He was put in charge of the newly formed 'A' Force, a body whose sole raison d'etre was deception. With the British numerically inferior in this theatre, anything they could do to create confusion in the enemy mind about their own dispositions or strength would be helpful. Clarke was exceptionally gifted and developed the concept of deception from scratch. He came to have a commanding understanding of how to make the enemy not just think, but to actually do what the Allies wanted them to. His former commander, Field Marshal Harold Alexander, was of the opinion that: 'He did as much to win the war as any other single officer.'[5]

One of Clarke's claims to fame was that he created the SAS. In January 1941 he had dressed two British soldiers in the uniform of a then-fictitious '1st Special Air Service' unit, and instructed them to go about Cairo talking loudly about missions to Crete or Libya. Later on, he was approached by a wounded Commando officer, David Stirling, who had the idea of creating small self-sufficient bands which operated independently behind enemy lines. He remembered:

> The name SAS came mainly from the fact I was anxious to get the full co-operation of a very ingenious individual called Dudley Clark[e], who was responsible for running a deception operation in Cairo ... Clark[e] was quite an influential chap and promised to give me all the help he could if I would use the name of his bogus brigade of parachutists, which is the Special Air Service, the SAS.[6]

The headquarters of 'A' Force was in a house of ill repute in one of the seedier parts of Cairo. It was also, as a cover for this highly secret work, tasked with training men in escape and evasion tactics, and in organising supplies for those who might need them. The arm that was to organise this work was known as 'N Section'. The head of this division from 21 September 1941 until the end of the war, was a regular soldier with an aptitude for intelligence work, Lieutenant Colonel A.C. (Tony) Simonds. Simonds had worked earlier in the war with the Special Operations Executive (SOE) and had learned a great deal about irregular methods of warfare. He also picked up a smattering of acquaintances in SOE with whom he would remain in contact for the remainder of the war, and on several occasions, this led to close and valuable co-operation in the field between SOE and MI9. In his memoirs, Simonds recalled:

> 'A' Force (MI9) was an Inter Service and Inter Allied organisation, devoted entirely to all aspects of escape and rescue work. [It] originated in September 1941, born out of the stress of two military disasters, Greece and Crete, [and] its task, scope and staff expanded enormously. I started in September with an office and one shorthand clerk. I collected escapers and evaders who were directed to the office for interrogation, and among the many volunteers to go back to the enemy lines to help their fellow escapers, I selected the best and most suitable. The secret was to grab such officers and O.R. volunteers before they had gone back to their units and been re-absorbed by the Military Machine.[7]

N Section had reason to be grateful to Dudley Clarke for the initial groundwork that he had laid when first establishing the station. He had for example taken the initiative in setting up the evasion lines across the Aegean, the key to which were two former British naval officers who had become consuls: Commander Vladimir Wolfson in Istanbul (Constantinople) and Lieutenant Commander Noël Rees in Izmir (Smyrna). Wolfson had both Jewish and Russian heritage and was resolutely anti-German. Rees, whose mother was Greek, came from one of the Anglo-Levantine families which dominated trade in the Middle East in this era. Rees had also been vice-consul in Chios, and knew the Dodecanese islands well. Not surprisingly he spoke excellent Greek, and in addition was married to a Greek wife. He was made British Vice Consul in Smyrna, and made his base in the old Rees family house in Boudjah (where he found on his arrival that his mother had left behind 27 cats and 18 dogs). The official account of the operation is held in War Office files, now declassified. There it is recorded that he successfully set up a secret operating base at Khioste, near Çesme, on the peninsula west of Izmir; a feat involving considerable bribery and personal influence. This clandestine naval facility at Khioste, just around the corner from the old holiday village of Lidjah, and opposite the island of Chios was to prove invaluable to the British. From Çesme, caiques were able to proceed to and from the coast of Turkey without let or hindrance. They continued to run throughout the war, in flagrant defiance of all existing laws in Turkey, and those applicable to neutral states. The selection of the peninsula of Çesme was a particularly happy choice in that it was a military area, where unauthorised persons could not proceed without permission, and except under most unusual circumstances, and no German or Italian agents succeeded in penetrating the peninsula throughout the entire war. It is fair to say that this base of Khioste, which was so successfully and amicably shared on an equal basis between MI9 and the Inter Service Liaison Department (ISLD) – a cover name used by MI6 – during the whole war would never have been established if it had not been for Rees.

From this clandestine base, it was not just the caiques of N Section which operated; as well as them, there were other odd craft, on even odder duties. N Section came to favour using escapers from enemy territory as its agents for forays into Axis-held areas, because the fact of being an escaper from an enemy prison camp could provide a cast-iron cover to account for one's presence at large in occupied territory. It was only believed necessary to have devoted time and thought to a watertight explanation of where one had been, and what one had been doing since the escape. The unpublished history of N Section records that:

> The first officer selected was Lieutenant Frank Macaskie, on the 10th October 1941 … at this time he was a lieutenant in the Leicestershire Regiment, who had carried out an extremely well organised escape, consisting of himself and three others, from Athens to Smyrna. The initiative displayed during this escape determined his selection. The first intention was, that after a short training with MI9 Cairo, he was to assist Mr Noël Rees in caique operations based on Smyrna … the services of the British officers and NCOs … were obtained through the co-operation of

> the DMI in attaching them to GSI for a short period of temporary duty, pending the revision of the A Force war establishment.[8]

Macaskie was issued with a false passport, which still survives in the possession of his family, in the name of his brother (though interestingly it carried his own date of birth, possibly in case he was questioned by a border official). It was further endorsed with a visa to enable him to enter Turkey. He reached Smyrna by aeroplane on 22 October 1941, two days earlier he had called again briefly on his friend Massey at Jerusalem. Although he had news about his activities in Cairo since his return from captivity, and informed him that he had been in contact with home via telegram, and had received supplies from both his mother and his girlfriend, he was unable to tell him anything of his future plans. However, we know from the unpublished history of 'A' Force that:

> After assisting Mr Noël Rees for some time on escape operations based on Smyrna … Macaskie produced several plans for returning to Athens. After considerable discussion as to the feasibility of these plans, and the likely dangers to be incurred, a plan (Caique Plan No1) was finally accepted after consultation with Commander Wolfson and Mr Noël Rees.
>
> Lieutenant Macaskie left for Athens at the end of November, to open up an escape route from Athens direct to Smyrna … he contacted all the heads of the

> voluntary escape organisations in Athens and laid a good foundation for future escape routes; and in particular put the voluntary organisations in the picture as to what was being done, both from Cairo and Smyrna.[9]

For reasons of security, and working on a need-to-know basis, three independent missions were initiated by MI9 in late 1941. Macaskie's was the first of the three to set off; once again dressed as a Greek fisherman, with codename 'Felix' and the temporary rank of captain, he returned to Greece on a special mission. On 20 November a British vessel carried him and his interpreter 21-year-old Alexis Ladas across the Mediterranean, and dropped them on the Greek coast. Ladas, a promising law student in Athens before the war, had been recruited by Macaskie and was now given the rank of Flight Sergeant in the Royal Hellenic Airforce. His additional role in the mission was to persuade as many influential Greeks as possible to support the exiled Greek government in Cairo rather than the Axis puppet regime in Athens. For context, it is worth noting that among the kaleidoscope of Greek political organisations there were those that although they were anti-Axis, also opposed the Monarchist government in exile. Ladas established himself at a safe house at 7 Prometheos Street in Marousi. Macaskie initially hid in a deserted house, from where he was picked up by Alexandros Levidis, a retired Hellenic naval commander who organised a loose association of former Greek officers willing to shelter British personnel, known initially as the Maleas group. Levidis had been alerted to the fact that Macaskie was back in Athens by Trypanis. He then stayed in a house on Skoufa Street, probably the boarding house of Mrs Smith (the Maltese widow of an Englishman, she would later be arrested for sheltering escaped prisoners of war). Macaskie lived and worked under the noses of Axis security forces, and even found himself in the cinema seated beside German officers. Because he was just as daring as during his previous stay in their capital, he was soon given the nickname 'O trelos' meaning 'The Crazy One', by the Greeks.

He seemed to thrive on danger, just as it seemed he did on love. Whatever his assertion to Massey on the troopship might have been, something had changed for Macaskie, as having just left a stormy illicit relationship in Smyrna to await his return, in Athens he found himself in a circle of young women who also sought love with him. More details of some of these women are known for sure, others not so. In November 1941 for example, Macaskie made contact with Mrs Titi Douka, an Athens woman who had helped him and another British officer the first time he escaped from captivity, and who aided him again now. She also assisted other British officers and for her efforts was imprisoned by the Italians for some months. Some published sources have stated that not only was she one of Macaskie's lovers, she was actually a high-class prostitute who also later consorted with German officers. However, documentation held by the UK National Archives and seen by the author would appear to conclusively refute this allegation. Be that as it may, the legend of Frank Macaskie as a spy and a hero was born in that chilly, wintery Athens in the last two months of 1941.

In his daring work he was assisted by Ladas, in spite of the orders he had received to cut off all contact with Macaskie as soon as they reached the outskirts of Athens. (Rees had pleaded with high-ranking SOE officer David Pawson to use an agent codenamed 'Odysseus' as Macaskie's guide to Athens. Pawson had categorically refused, lest his valuable asset be endangered. It was then agreed that Ladas would lead Macaskie instead, but only to the fringes of the city, whereupon all his obligations would cease.) With Ladas as an interpreter, Macaskie initially put Levidis in contact with Epameinondas Tsellos (a retired army officer and former government minister) and Theodoros Kountouriotis (the son of one of Greece's most famous admirals), who entrusted him with receiving the information they collected, cross-checking it and sending it, by whatever means he had, to Noël Rees, and that continued until money and a wireless set were sent to them. At the same time, he visited the leaders or executives of other refugee organisations, such as Zanna, run by Colonel Alexandros ('Alex') Melas, a close friend of Noël Rees and a member of the British secret services. Macaskie reorganised Trypanis's group, just as he also reorganised the rudimentary espionage organisation that Tsellos had created – on instructions from Smyrna – with Colonels Konstantinos Dovas and Stylianos Kitrilakis at the helm. The new organisation – the joint creation of Noël Rees and Macaskie – was to be codenamed 'Homer', as it originated in the poet's most likely birthplace, Smyrna. Henceforth, the militarily organised 'Homer' was financed mainly by ISLD. Initially, its agents were of all political shades, even communists. However, the leadership drifted gradually rightwards with most of its leaders being royalists. When the divisions between different political factions in Greece began to grow, the persons who belonged to or wanted to join leftist organisations discreetly moved away.

'Homer', with successive leaders Tsellos and Kitrilakis, was gradually developing into the most serious espionage and counter-espionage organisation that the Axis faced. Its actions initially extended over a large part of Greece, while later, by order of Smyrna, it was limited mainly to Attica, Evia and Corinth. 'Homer', moreover, was not troubled by the kind of internal disputes and betrayals that afflicted, with many victims, the 'Apollon' group of Giannis Peltekis, the other major espionage organisation, the one under the control of SOE. (It is also interesting to observe that the kaleidoscopic nature of the Greek resistance, with its many rival organisations, found a mirror in the equally fractured and competitive world of British intelligence, with each service adopting a different group.)

Homer's regular communication – via radio – with Smyrna took place three times a week, which developed, during the last two months of the Occupation, into daily contact. Its informants were recruited in the port of Piraeus, in the SEK (ΣΕΚ – Hellenic State Railways), and in state and German services. They channelled information to the organisation not just about construction projects, about the movements of enemy ships and trains, but also about agents that the Germans sent to the Middle East from Athens, one of their main bases for this purpose. Finally, there was one more service that 'Homer' offered, this one in the context of the activities of 'A' Force: it succeeded in recruiting some of these enemy operatives as double agents, apparently acting on behalf of the Germans, in order for them to send back false information after their arrival in the Middle East. These same agents were used after the Liberation by Allied intelligence to send misleading information to the enemy. As for the casualties suffered by the organisation, seven of its informants were executed by the Germans, four were murdered by communist paramilitaries, two disappeared and one, after being tortured by the Germans, continued his activities as a sailing ship captain but died soon from the injuries he had suffered.

In December 1941 Evgenios Valasakis, now leader of a third resistance organisation, the Maleas group, received a visit from two 'Cypriot' agents of the British secret services, who were none other than Macaskie and Ladas. (As late as 1951, in a report he was asked by the Greek government to prepare, Valasakis was not allowed to use their names and so invented the 'Cypriot' guise.) The purpose of the visit was to give him a letter from Noël Rees asking him for information on the activities of his organisation up to then. At the same time, Rees entreated him to intercede so that the two 'Cypriots' could visit Themistocles Sofoulis (head of the Liberal Party) and Georgios Kafantaris (leader of the Progressive Party), to ask them to take charge of the resistance, or to direct it, or, failing this, to leave for Egypt, so that they could join the Greek government. The failure of these visits left a bitter memory for all concerned; Sofoulis was negative on all three occasions that they met him. Valasakis recounted his reaction, based on the argument that participation of the mainstream political parties in the resistance would deprive Greece of political leadership after its liberation:

> Themistocles Sofoulis listened to me carefully and was quick to react to what I told him. 'What are these things?' he told me. 'Since when do parties take over the organisation of national resistance movements? What are you asking me? We cannot represent the conspirators. These are jobs for others, not for us. What the Cairo government and the Middle East Headquarters are asking for is not only dangerous but could also be disastrous. I stress this to you: It is not the work of the parties to lead the resistance. Because this could cause an unprecedented backlash against the political leadership and against the candidates. And the leaders and officials of the parties are known to everyone. Imagine what will happen and what will follow. The parties will experience irreparable dissolution. If the parties disappear after the liberation, Greece will find itself in a very difficult position.'[10]

The meeting with Kafantaris took place in a small house next to the Panathinaikos Stadium, in the presence of resistance leader Grigorios Lambrakis and other political figures. Whilst not a communist, Lambrakis certainly had leftwing views. The reaction was the same, with the only difference being that Kafantaris, more theoretical than Sofoulis, characterised the parties as 'surface organisations', because they were visible from everywhere and thus were more vulnerable than 'underground' ones. The only one left to meet now was leader of the Omiros resistance group Panagiotis Kanellopoulos. Macaskie listened to his views on the Greek resistance and forwarded Noël Rees's request for a report on Greek matters. Ladas also brought him the same offer to join the exiled leadership in Cairo, only to receive the stereotypical negative response, supplemented by the remark: 'Besides, I have not received an official invitation from the Greek government...'

The chief reason for the overwhelmingly lukewarm response to the overtures of Macaskie and Ladas was the yawning gulf between the Greek government in exile, and the majority of the population left behind under occupation. If the politicians and resistance leaders were largely hostile to the government, this was because of the attitude of the government itself, which to a considerable extent viewed the resistance as the work of irresponsible radicals who were a threat to the country's future. Rather than making every effort to encourage or direct home grown resistance activity, politicians in the Greek cabinet were at best indifferent and at worst openly hostile to resistance activity. The Prime Minister in exile, Emmanouil Tsouderos, was also viewed with suspicion by many politicians who had chosen to remain behind, who regarded him as too close to the unpopular King George II; he in turn was seen as the facilitator of the pre-war Greek dictatorship of Ioannis Metaxas.

A little later Macaskie supplied Valasakis with a radio that had arrived from Smyrna, complete with instructions and code. He also handed him 100 gold pounds and the second letter from Noël Rees, who informed Valasakis that he was now to act on orders from Allied HQ. Rees asked him to re-establish contact with him immediately, and to man a small boat to send his information reports to Smyrna (at this time it was far more dangerous to transmit from a clandestine radio than it was to receive). Valasakis' wireless would receive the code name 'PEA 1', while 'PEA 2' was to be the name of a second device that he would receive later. Thus, in February 1942, Valasakis' espionage and counter-espionage organisation was 'officially' recognised by the British, under the codename 'Aliki', which in Cairo was referred to as the Valasakis - Lambrakis - Doxiadis organisation. (The origin of the name 'Aliki' is uncertain. It was the name of Noël Rees's wife, but it was also that of Valasakis's first wife, now dead, to whom he was devoted.) 'Aliki' extended to many parts of Greece, from Thessaloniki to Heraklion in Crete and from Chios to Patras. A boat with sails - later to be equipped with an engine in Smyrna - transported the information sheets, while from August 1942 Valasakis disappeared from the residence he had occupied at 22 Anagnostopoulou Street, and hid in various friends' houses, always using a pseudonym. At the same time, he also filed a divorce action, in order to absolve his wife of any responsibility in the eyes of the enemy's prosecuting services. Until the strengthening of 'Homer', the 'Aliki' organisation was the main espionage network in Greece. As for the reports containing political content sent to Smyrna, their authenticity was certified by their signature either by Lambrakis or by Archbishop Chrysanthos who was involved with the resistance. As Levidis later wrote, at the end of December 1941 he would also receive funds – Macaskie gave him 800,000 drachmas i.e. 40 gold pounds, at the then exchange rate of the gold pound against the undervalued drachma – which were loans from Alexander Paspatis who owned the Bank of Chios and who financed his operations.

The ill-prepared British attempt to prop up Greece in many ways resembled her efforts to do the same thing in Norway, a year earlier. It ended in a humiliating debacle, and in the chaotic withdrawal of British, Australian and New Zealand troops many were left behind. Macaskie's mission was also to contact these men and with the help of the Greek resistance, to guide them to the coast and return them to British lines. The only flaw in this plan was that many of the Allied soldiers who had thus far evaded Axis captivity were reluctant to leave Greece. Unlike officers, whose duty was wherever possible to try to escape, many of the other ranks were less eager. Having endured the hardships and privations of the Greek campaign, many had been taken in by Greek families or were hiding in the hills and were being supplied by them. Unlike the hard tack and bully beef of their army rations they now had (at least until the famine which struck Greece in the winter of 1941/1942) access to good food, fine wines and in some cases even the attention of local women. No wonder they were somewhat reluctant to rejoin the war! Nevertheless Macaskie managed to get some 250 out of the country successfully. At the time there were no less than four escape organisations functioning in Athens alone, and that of George Trypanis with the assistance of Macaskie became extremely effective as recorded by the unpublished history of 'A' Force. It notes the fact that the British officer had considerable success in improving this network, that is until Trypanis was compromised, and Macaskie was forced to evacuate him.

One day in December 1941 the tramways manager Thomashausen had called Trypanis into his office, and had shown him an anonymous letter accusing him of collaborating with the British. Trypanis realised that to stay in Greece would endanger his life and decided to escape to the Middle East, together with his wife Besy Adosidou. However because there were others who also had to leave, the preparations were time-consuming. Finally, a boat was secured – it was bought with money from a wealthy resistance sympathiser – and Ilias Chrysinis, part of the organisation of Lela Karagiannis, was chosen as its captain. The fugitives, moreover, were divided into two parties. Macaskie was to be accompanied by a disparate group comprising Alexis Ladas, the Trypanis couple, Alexandros Kriekoukias, and Georgios Paspatis (an Athenian student of English who was later awarded an MC and MiD, after becoming the lieutenant and skipper of an SOE caique with the Anglo-Hellenic Schooner Squadron). Georgios was also the son of Alexander Paspatis. As well as these, Lieutenant Filippos Messinezis made up the group. Another team was to wait for them in Lavrio, with the skipper who carried the mail for 'Homer' and the supplies for the trip. The fake shipping documents were supplied by the harbour vice-captain Nikos Stambolis, later an executive of 'Aliki', whilst fake identities were delivered by the Athens police chief Aggelos Evert (whose codenames were 'Otto', and 'Skylark'.) Now Macaskie, dressed as a fisherman, was to be known as George Lily.

Also among this escape party was a Royal Army Service Corps driver named Francis Jones, from Liverpool. Jones had no desire to spend the war in an Italian prison camp, and on one particular hot and dusty march had taken the opportunity to slip away from his less than vigilant captors.

He made contacts among the local Greek civilians who were largely sympathetic to escaped PoWs. Gradually he was passed through the networks of the Greek resistance until he arrived in Piraeus on the escape route for British prisoners. It was Christmas Eve, 1941 and he was led to a safe house near the waterfront. Taken upstairs, he was ushered into the presence of four English speaking Greeks – the leaders of the local partisans. They were George Trypanis, the senior man, Alexis Ladas, and Panagiotis Kanellopoulos who had been educated in England since childhood. The fourth man was Georgios Paspatis. Jones was grilled for several minutes in his own language, but having lived among Greeks for a number of months and having thought and spoken only in that language, he found abruptly switching back to English difficult. When they questioned him in Greek, ironically he found it easier; the quartet were entitled to be cautious however, for they knew that someone in their organisation was leaking information to the Gestapo. Having passed the interrogation, he sat down next to an Englishman in a sports jacket and introduced himself. His compatriot then revealed that it was actually he who was in charge there, and he had been watching Jones' mannerisms during the entire interrogation to assess if he was genuine. It was his first meeting with Frank Macaskie. Jones wrote later:

> At first it puzzled me why such men as the Georges-Alexis-Panagiotis quartet accepted him as a leader. They looked far brainier and more ruthless than he did. But for the alert eyes in his rather sleepy face Macaskie looked a stodgy individual. It was the impression he liked to give.

> It was also one of his greatest assets. For underneath this cloak of amiable nonentity was shrewdness and astonishing courage. Frank Macaskie already had a reputation that any officer in the Middle East would have envied: ahead of him lay exploits that were to win him the title of 'Scarlet Pimpernel of Greece.'[11]

Macaskie's escape route would in time become highly effective, but in its early stages, when still in its infancy, teething troubles were not uncommon. For example, the Gestapo had noticed Macaskie's boat in Piraeus harbour, and had grown suspicious and confiscated it. Undaunted, he had purchased another, and tried to stay one step ahead of the Germans. Before dawn the following morning the fugitives were leaving the safehouse for the quayside in pairs, to avoid attracting undue scrutiny. To board here would attract too much attention however, so they continued beyond the harbour to a remote spot at the foot of a cliff, about a quarter of a mile away. Even here there was danger, as a lone German sentry patrolled above. The boat was signalled by torch, and in the semi-darkness a shabby, dilapidated hull became slowly visible. With no engine, heavily patched sails and about six inches of bilge in the bottom it looked an unlikely craft to be transporting escaped PoWs to Turkey, but its unprepossessing appearance meant that the Germans would let it come and go as it pleased – for the most part. Yet, as Macaskie ruefully observed later: 'We were bound to be caught sooner or later, for all Athens knew when a caique was leaving.'[12]

What was to follow over the next eighteen months would test Macaskie's resolve and character to their limits; the at times brutal and degrading treatment that he was to receive, particularly at the hands of the Italians, would leave its mark for the remainder of his life. Yet even in the face of almost certain death the fortitude and sheer courage that he displayed were to be an inspiration to those with him.

Chapter Four

Disaster and Defiance

It must have been hard to imagine a stranger Christmas Day as the Macaskie party set off from Athens to a clandestine rendezvous with the motorboat, the *Moulis*. Chrysinis, the skipper of the motorboat, with his secret contingent from Lavrio had authority from the Germans to go to the island of Samos. On the way, he would drop his illicit human cargo on the Turkish shore at Smyrna – provided of course that he could dodge the two Italian patrol boats which regularly monitored this coastline. The skipper of the sailing boat must have been under no illusion about how reckless the undertaking was. In a vessel this poor, the journey would have been difficult in the summer, with a sea like a millpond. In the depths of winter in temperatures near freezing it was sheer folly. On the way the sea got rougher and rougher. Waves began to crash over the gunwales and Macaskie was not the only one leaning over the side to be sick, losing his hat in the process.

Despite the choppy sea the other boatman was alert and was straining his eyes into the distance. All at once he sprang to life, waving his arms and instructing the passengers to get down. Almost as one they slipped off the seats and crouched in the bottom of the boat, oblivious to the bilge which now lapped around their waists. Half a mile in the distance, a destroyer was coming in from the open sea, and as it passed by at full speed about a furlong distant, a great wall of wash raced away from its bow towards the boatful of fugitives. It pitched and rocked, but the passengers remained hidden and the danger passed. With a strong wind behind them, they had every chance of crossing the forty miles of water to their island rendezvous by lunchtime, but these waters can be temperamental. The half gale subsided as suddenly as it had blown up, and now under a hot sun the sail which had previously billowed from the mast hung lifelessly. The sea was flat calm. Once or twice the clandestine cargo were forced to hide in the bilge again, but each time the approaching vessel turned out to be Greek and the danger passed. As dusk fell, the breeze began to pick up again, slowly at first, but soon enough to fill the sails and once more they were on their way.

They arrived at the island, Tselevinia, an hour after dark. The boatman left immediately and the launch taking them onward was not due until first light. Thus the party climbed up to the highest ground, where a small stone hut (a former Greek Orthodox chapel) was to be their shelter for the night. In the cold of December, with an icy draught blowing through, the evening was an uncomfortable one and Macaskie was up before dawn, looking for any sign of the launch. Several boats appeared on the horizon, but hopes were dashed each time as they sailed past. At mid-day there was still nothing, and by three in the afternoon they were growing concerned. Perhaps the crew had been arrested, but this seemed unlikely as the boat's papers were all in order – they had been prepared by Georgios Trypanis. A mechanical breakdown seemed equally unlikely as Macaskie had given the skipper enough money to buy a whole second engine in spare parts, and there were also two mechanics among the crew.

The non-appearance meant another freezing night in the stone hut, and this time a fierce gale sprang up. By morning it was so strong that there was no possibility of a small craft going out in it. For two days the wind screamed around the shelter and the sound of waves crashing on the rocks below the summit provided the mood music. The provisions that they had brought with them ran out, and the escape party survived on boiled cabbage and potatoes, scrounged from the local peasants, a nearby village being accessed via a narrow causeway at low tide. The vegetables were welcome, but none of the villagers had any cigarettes, causing hardship for the smokers. On the first day they re-lit stubs and dog-ends. On the second, they were in a foul mood and resorted to lighting grass and herbs but nothing proved successful. One even experimented with dried sheep's dung as a substitute for tobacco. It burnt well, and initially hopes were high, but it proved too rank! The low mood of the smokers soon affected everyone, and on the third day it rained hard to further add to the misery. The hut proved to be a leaky one, and hopes of a successful escape were fading fast.

The sky darkened and the rain increased to torrential proportions, when a strange figure appeared in the doorway of the hut. He introduced himself by throwing down a packet of Papastratos No 7 cigarettes, which for the smokers was the equivalent of manna from Heaven. This man was a New Zealander sapper named Roy Spencer Natusch, and he had a remarkable but at the same time familiar tale to tell. He too had been captured in Greece, but had also escaped from the Germans. Since then, he had been wandering around the Peloponnese trying to steal a boat or make contact with an Allied agent. Having almost been recaptured and shot at whilst trying to steal an Italian MTB, he fled inland, where he heard rumours about Macaskie's band being nearby. This was concerning in itself for the escape party, but they nonetheless made him welcome, especially as he had brought cigarettes.

The next morning the storm had blown itself out and warmer weather arrived. With it came the long-awaited rescue launch. The party ran whooping down to the water's edge to meet it – all that is except Macaskie, who was not one to show excitement. With the boat was Chrysinis, who explained that the delay had been caused initially by a two-day ban on sailings imposed by the Germans, and then the storm which had caused further inconvenience. Fortunately he had the presence of mind to bring extra stocks of food and cigarettes with him. After dark that night, New Year's Eve 1941, their motor powered caique set sail for Turkey, but it was a sad departure for they left without one of the Greek members of the party, whose task it was to return to Athens and report to the resistance what had happened. They left him waving from the cliffs and soon the diesel-engined boat was chugging along at a steady ten knots, with Chrysinis at the wheel, guiding it between the islands. He knew the route well, and exactly where the patrol boats would be; he intended to slip between them when they were at the farthest ends of their beat. It was now just 160 miles to Smyrna. The island of Kea loomed ahead, and was soon receding into the distance.

The safety of the shores of Asia Minor seemed to be at hand, but after many hours at sea, as it neared the Turkish coast the motor of their craft suddenly stopped running. At once a cluster of concerned faces appeared in the small engine room. The vessel was out of fuel, but Chrysinis assured them that it was simply a case of switching fuel tanks and they would be on their way again in two minutes. Two minutes became ten, and then twenty. With the tank now replenished, the engine refused to start. If it did not fire up soon, they would have to go back, as the danger from the now returning patrol boats grew ever greater. Next, they discovered that the compressed air bottles needed to re-start the quickly cooling diesel engine were empty, and frantically now the three sailors tried to turn the heavy motor over by hand. However, the enormous compression of the cylinders was too much for them. With no mechanical propulsion the vessel and her occupants were left drifting and at the mercy of the elements, for the sea and wind now decided to conspire against them; a fierce breeze picked up and the boat began to bob around like a cork. With motor power she could have pressed on through the waves, but now she was drifting. In desperation they ran up a sail, but during the night the wind had turned to the east and began taking them back the way they had come, towards Greece.

In the breaking light of New Year's Day the group found themselves again near the island of Kythnos, which they had passed hours before, and by early afternoon they drifted into one of the island's coves, where they beached the boat. Almost immediately the postmortem over the debacle began, with one of the Greeks demanding that Chrysinis explain exactly what had just happened. The guilty look on his face told the others all they needed to know, but with further prompting he admitted that he had been so confident in his boat that he had not bothered to spend the money that he had been given on spares, but instead he and his crew went on a monumental three-day drinking binge. Probably because they were hung over, and didn't bother to check, they left Piraeus with the fuel tanks half full and only one bottle of compressed air. Apportioning blame however was not going to fix the problem, and at this point Macaskie took charge. He knew that the island, like most of any size, would have an Italian garrison, so they had to work fast before they were discovered. He sent Chrysinis to a village to try to secure a blow lamp – if they could heat the top of the engine up sufficiently, then they might be able to hand start it. If no blow lamp could be found, they would knock the bottom out of a bucket, put it on top of the engine and fill it with hot coals. As a last resort some of the party also started making another sail, in order to try to reach Turkey once the wind changed.

Just before dark, Chrysinis returned, waving the blowlamp triumphantly above his head. Macaskie's last words to him before setting off had been to try to keep a low profile, but he had evidently stayed in the tavern where the deal was done to celebrate with the locals, who were now probably fully aware of the purpose for which it was needed. They could not leave until next morning, when the patrol boats would be once more at extreme range, so the party spent the night in another stone hut, near the beach. It was warmer than their previous abode, but unfortunately it was also infested with fleas. Everyone was bitten, but nonetheless morale was rising once more as the prospect of getting underway again beckoned. At first light the Greeks were aboard the vessel, working on the engine. It promised to be a long job but the warmth of the sun and the peace of the tranquil bay in which they lay lulled them into a false sense of security. Without warning, a chug-chug-chug heralded the sudden approach of a small ship around the headland. Macaskie, Jones and Natusch were still on the beach at this point, and the former at once ordered the other two to run. Pounding up the sand towards the cover of some hillocks, shots rang out and bullets passed over their heads. From the cover of the higher ground they counted fifteen Italian soldiers on the beach, none of whom clearly was a first-class shot. Desperate to find safety they headed further inland, climbing a steep bluff. When they reached the top, Jones breathless and exhausted but Macaskie and Natusch (a former All-Black) proving much fitter, they realised that the Italians had given up the pursuit. With the boat crew under armed guard, they fixed a tow-rope behind their patrol vessel and headed off. Three Greeks had been sent to fetch water, and thus also avoided being captured. Alerted by the shooting, they stayed low until the Italians had left. Two decided to leave and headed home by themselves. The third, a young Athenian named Costas chose to join the Macaskie party. Macaskie now summed up the situation, Jones remembering his words many years later:

> There were fifteen Wops down there, at a guess I'd say there's about fifty in the garrison. They'll hunt us,

> I expect, but we've got the advantage. The islanders'll be on our side. If it comes to a push we should get a boat from them. That's if we need it of course. But we'll have to see about the others first. Maybe we can help them. Perhaps we'll get our own back. It's worth a try, anyway. Tell the Greek, Bill, will you?[1]

As Jones related what Macaskie had told him to Costas, he saw the colour drain from his face. Although Natusch was also keen to try to rescue the prisoners, for the other two the prospect of taking on armed Italian guards seemed like a suicide mission. Nevertheless they went along with it as, for several nights, they dodged sentries and spied out the garrison headquarters where the rest of the contingent were being held. Eventually it became clear that without taking out the entire garrison – realistically the task of a full-strength commando unit – there would be no way of freeing them from their cells in the main building. Macaskie was no fool, and despite his disappointment agreed that they should call off the rescue attempt.

Little did he know that, shortly after they had parted, the Greeks had managed to convince their Italian captors (including a very young and obviously frightened officer) that they were merely travellers who had left the mainland, ravaged as it was by food shortages, in search of provisions. Initially they had been believed, and their captivity had been quite relaxed. After a couple of days, however they had been taken away by boat once more to the Vafiadaki prison on Syros, where they were led, chained, to the offices of the notorious CS (Contra Spionaggio) the Italian counter-espionage arm.

There their luck changed dramatically. Besy Adosidou flirted with the Italians and – it is said out of sheer stupidity, though she may simply have been frightened – revealed to them not only the names of the fugitives but also the true identity of Macaskie, with the additional information that he had come from Smyrna. The Italians, not wishing to inflict the hardships of prison on her, sent her instead to the hospital. In order to cover for her, Trypanis would write in his report after the war that he was the one who confessed everything during the interrogation.

Macaskie meanwhile had to come up with a new plan. He now decided that they would sail back to the mainland, walk to Athens, re-equip there and then try again to reach Turkey. This however also had its risks. Ideally they would use a motorboat, but if necessary they were prepared to row across the 30-mile stretch of sea. This, they had no doubt, would be no picnic. If one of the sudden January storms were to blow up, in an open boat they would stand little chance. Even if the weather were to be clement, however hard they rowed they estimated that it could still take ten hours. Then there was the risk of being intercepted whilst at sea, but this danger had to be faced; they could not stay on Kythnos indefinitely. The obvious place from which to depart was Merika, a small fishing village on the west coast of the island. Here the Italians kept one of their two patrol boats. According to friendly villagers only eight men guarded it. As well as advice, the locals provided food that they could ill afford to spare (for great shortages also affected the Greek islands this winter), lodgings, and warnings of any approaching Italian patrol. Frank remembered this later: 'I saw the famine in the winter of 1941, when people were dying in the streets [of Athens], and ate grass and thistles myself, but everyone would share with me what he had; I have had nothing but kindness from these people.'[2]

For this sleepy island, this was perhaps the most exciting thing that had happened in many years. For the evaders, if their luck held, they would be away before the alarm was raised and there would be no one to pursue them. The only other motorboat was on the other side of the island, and they could be halfway to the mainland before it put to sea. Even a general alert along the coast would not help the Italians, for if they landed in darkness and sank the boat, no one would be any the wiser. As they waited for night to fall, hiding in a barn, Jones was in high spirits – the rescue mission was off and he thought his chances on the seas were about even. Macaskie however was disconsolate, and not just because he had run out of cigarettes once again. Mainly, he was disappointed in himself because he believed he had let down his friends. Costas the Greek however was clearly terrified, and no words or reassurance could console him. The decision was taken that it was better all round if they left him, and just before midnight the two Englishmen and New Zealander came out of the barn and crept silently down to the shore. The half-moon in the sky shone a weak light on a line of small boats on the beach. Some they noted had oars – useful in case there was need of a back-up plan. Now Natusch took off his shoes and headed away quietly to inspect the motorboat. He moved like a ghost, but even so one or two of the village dogs had already let out an inquisitive bark. Any more noise from the beach, and there would be a raucous chorus of them. Minutes passed by, and the tension rose, until Natusch reappeared, and immediately shattered their hopes. The motorboat was there, and the engine was still warm. It would probably fire up at once, but a dipstick in the fuel tank had revealed that it was almost empty.

The trio now realised that they had to return to the rowing boats, and after minutes of discussion decided to row to the adjacent island of Kea, a distance of approximately 20 kilometres, and use it as a stepping stone to the mainland, sinking the boat when they got there. The debate was cut short however by a voice in the darkness. 'Viene qua!' it called out, followed by, 'Alt, mani in alto!' Presently the owner of the voice appeared from the darkness, a squat Italian guard, waving his rifle menacingly from side to side. The village dogs had woken him, and he had decided to investigate. As the trio put their hands up, he switched to Greek, asking them what they were doing. For a moment it appeared that he had not realised that they were English. Jones replied in Greek, hoping to convince him that he was a fisherman who had forgotten that his oars had been left in his boat, and had come to retrieve them, along with his two brothers. The fact that all three were in their socks only added to the guard's suspicions, however and he switched back to Italian and ordered them towards the guard room, fifty yards away. For Jones and Natusch, any previous optimism now evaporated, and to them it appeared that the game was up.

They had reckoned without Macaskie, however. Lagging at the back, he made a pretence of dropping his shoe then scrambling around on the ground to retrieve it. As he did so, the unwary guard closed the distance between them. Keeping low under the barrel of the rifle, Macaskie now made a lunge for his legs. As they wrestled for the weapon, it went off, the report shattering the night. The guard, convinced that he had been shot, let out a piercing shriek and fled. Not surprisingly every dog in Merika was now in full voice and in the houses, lights were coming on. The Italian garrison would soon be out in force and it was every man for himself as the trio fled.

They managed to find each other again close to the barn that they had departed from earlier that night; Macaskie true to his character was a picture of *sang froid*, and completely unruffled by the earlier events. At any rate, that was the impression that he gave to the others. More importantly, he still had the rifle that he had won in the struggle with the guard. After searching fruitlessly for Costas, the trio set off up a track into the hinterland. The moon having set, they were now in pitch darkness. After walking some distance, Macaskie lost his footing and went over a precipice. He fell ten feet, but managed a complete somersault and landed upright, unharmed. By a miracle, the rifle neither went off accidentally nor impaled him. This time however his demeanour was different, and as the two others hauled him back up onto the track he had a few choice words to say about the darkness, the rifle and the Italians. At this they broke into a smile. By now the garrison was in action on the road below them, as evidenced by the headlights of the trucks and the crack of rifles as the soldiers fired at what they thought was movement, but which in reality was probably a flock of startled sheep.

The three escapers left them to it. It was now certain that they would have to leave Kythnos, for it had become much too hot for them; they would have to find a rowing boat and get to nearby Saros, even though it was in the wrong direction. The next day, all was quiet. The Italians had returned to barracks. More ominous however was the complete lack of boats. The Greek inhabitants had all heard about the battle of the previous night and were eager to press food and wine onto their guests, but none would admit to owning a boat. At last an elderly man agreed that he had a spare one, but the only snag was that his son was out fishing in it, and would not be back until six that evening. Macaskie and Natusch were suspicious. Only Jones, who spoke better Greek, believed the old man, and so they agreed to part company. This made sense in any event, as the Italians were looking for three men. Macaskie, still with the rifle hidden under his long coat, might stand a better chance with just one companion.

He and Natusch now tried to double bluff the Italians by returning to their headquarters, and trying to steal the patrol boat which was housed there. By this point however the commandante was alert, and had posted extra sentries and a search light. It was a non-starter so they tried for a local boat, but again the commandante was ahead of them, and had ordered all Greek boatmen in the vicinity to remove oars and rowlocks. The disconsolate duo broke into the island's only hotel, which was closed for the duration, and at least had a good night's sleep on spring mattresses. After that, they hid out in a barn once more as another storm battered the island for twenty-four hours. At this point, the local bush telegraph brought them back together with Jones, who had exciting news. Nicos, the farmer who was sheltering him, had a brother who regularly came over from Samos. He was due that night, and under cover of darkness would spirit them away. Again, they allowed their hopes to rise, but predictably as so often before the boat failed to materialise. Nicos was almost at the point of tears with disappointment, but the others consoled him and thanked him for his hospitality before moving on.

They now sat and reviewed the situation. For a week now they had been trying to escape from this island, and had been dogged by nothing but bad luck at each attempt. The jinx went back even further if one included the catastrophe that had landed them in this pickle in the first place! There was nothing for it however but to keep trying, and an hour later they spotted a likely craft, a small white yacht moored in an isolated bay. Natusch went to investigate, and even managed to avoid the ubiquitous Greek dogs, but found the crew were still aboard. The trio weighed up the risks, and decided not to chance a confrontation. This boat was not for them. Another night was spent sheltering in one of the many tiny stone churches which dotted the island, before another small cove revealed a fishing hamlet of just two dwellings, and a boat being rowed in towards the shore. The occupants went into one of the houses, taking the oars with them – which was only to be expected, given the events of the week just passed. Jones and Natusch went inside to negotiate for the boat, whilst Macaskie waited outside with the rifle.

Jones tried at first to be reasonable, explaining the situation, and the fact that they would leave a promissory note for 50,000 drachmas to be honoured after the war. He even explained that as they were leaving, they would fire a shot in the air which everyone around would hear, so that they could claim the boat was taken from them by force. The Greeks however were having none of it, and appeared terrified of the Italians. In the end Jones scrawled out the note, the two escapers grabbed the oars and pushed their way out past them. As they did so, Macaskie fired a shot into the air; pandemonium now ensued. Amid the screams and shouts of the Greeks, one claimed he had a pistol. That set the three Allied escapers running into the darkness, not realising that the field leading down to the shore was terraced. As they fell over, Macaskie, who had reloaded, accidentally fired again, just missing Natusch. They reached the boat as the commotion behind them was dying away, and pushed it out into the surf. At last, they were on their way – or so they thought.

Macaskie decided to get well out away from the shore before beginning the journey to Kea. They had the length of Kythnos to cover – some ten miles – plus the open stretch between the two islands, some 25 miles all told. They felt the odds were now in their favour however, as they had a sound boat, calm waters and ten hours of darkness ahead of them. Yet the perfect conditions were in some ways a double-edged sword, as the sea was full of phosphorescence which lit the boat up like moonlight. As it was, Macaskie's decision to head out proved a wise one, for shortly afterwards, their ears picked up a sound in the inky blackness ahead. They stopped rowing. Gradually it became clearer – the ominous 'chug chug' of the patrol vessel. Macaskie whispered to them to get down, and they crouched silently in the bottom of the skiff. Evidently the Italians had heard the shots and had decided to investigate. The motor boat drew nearer and seemed to be heading towards them, until suddenly it veered to pass between them and the shore. Searchlights were combing the rocky coast and dark figures could be seen aboard the ship, looking inland. In the darkness the rowing boat blended with the crags that jutted out of the sea nearby, and the patrol boat continued its progress until out of sight around the next headland.

They reached the northern tip of Kythnos at 1.00 am, with the sea still glassy and calm. Natusch however was worried; a keen yachtsman himself, he knew a thing or two about the weather. He was sure high winds were coming, but the others dismissed him. In any case, they could hardly go back to where they had come from, and pressed on towards Kea. The weather broke when they were about 6 miles out. The unpredictable nature of the Aegean in winter was proved beyond doubt when, in just over ten minutes it turned from flat calm to full gale force conditions. The wind came at them like a fury, sending great crests of waves crashing over them. One set of oars was snatched away by the wind, and hurled into the night. As Macaskie and Jones baled furiously, Natusch used all his powers of seamanship at the tiller, trying to ride the vessel over crests and keeping her head into the wind. For two hours he fought with all the strength that he had, and then, as suddenly as it had started, the storm miraculously abated. Despite their tiredness, again the men began to row. However they had reckoned without the current, which was now carrying them down the channel between the islands, rather than across it. The effort of rowing now left them dripping with sweat, and progress was desperately slow. As dawn broke, they were still half a mile from shore, and the rays of the early morning sun revealed in front of them a gleaming white coastguard building, covering the southern tip of Kea.

After a final effort the boat crested the surf and beached at the foot of the cliff beneath the coastguard building. As the exhausted men jumped out, awaiting them were two Italian marines, with levelled carbines. They were calm, almost friendly in their demeanour. Their commander however was a different story. Short and officious, he spoke a little Greek, and Jones tried to convince him that they were just fishermen, but it was a lost cause. No Greek fishermen were likely to turn up without nets or other equipment in the middle of a January gale. Their very presence on Kea was suspicious, and the Italian rifle in the bottom of the boat did nothing to help their story. Under the command of the officer the party now marched off the beach, Macaskie still carrying his rifle but now devoid of bolt and cartridges. The track was rough, and his footwear was in a poor state. Before long it had disintegrated, and he tried to carry on for a while in bare feet, but it was no use. With his feet cut and bloodied by the sharp stones of the path, he sat down. The other two joined him, and despite the shouting of the guards, there they remained, Macaskie pointing at his feet and explaining in broken Italian that he could go no further like that. At this the guards raised their rifles, took careful aim, and began counting backwards. Refusing still to move, Macaskie let out a guffaw (it was, recalled Jones, the only time he had ever heard him laugh). At that distance even an Italian soldier could hardly miss, but it was obvious that it was all a bluff. The prisoners were too big a prize for the officer to be shot out of hand, and they all knew it. Eventually one of the guards went off, and came back with a mule for Macaskie to ride. He thanked him courteously, and the journey continued.

It was at least ten miles to the garrison headquarters, and by the time they got there the commandante was in wireless communication with Kythnos, getting a full update on their activities on that island. Jones was first to be interrogated; Macaskie had advised him to offer only his name rank and number, and the fact that he was an escaped PoW from Greece. The commandante, dressed as flamboyantly as any Italian officer could be, strode around the room, dog whip in hand, lashing out at the furniture. The first questions from the interpreter were in Greek, which Jones pretended not to understand. When he replied in English, the commandate's eyebrows lifted and he stopped pacing. These men were bigger fish than he had imagined. When a couple of blows from the dog whip failed to produce any answers to his questions, he turned his attention to Macaskie. When he discovered that he was a captain, he knew he might really be onto something. Producing his trump card, the fake Greek identity paper which he had found on him, he added: 'You say you're a British officer, but you're in civilian clothing and you have this passport. That makes you a spy. Well, you know the usual treatment. Spies are shot. Tell me, are you an agent?'[3]

Technically he was, but Macaskie was unruffled and after the guileless reminder about shooting he was hardly going to admit to it. He reiterated to the officer the cover story that they were all escaped PoWs, and not spies. The fake document meant nothing, as any prisoner on the run in Greece could have picked one up from the resistance. Then he posed the question – would three spies really have turned up in a boat, half drowned, with no equipment? For in spite of their searches, tearing out linings of clothing and pulling apart shoes, the guards had found not a single item indicating espionage. At the end of a long and weary day, in which they had had nothing at all to eat, the fugitives were finally given soup and bread. They ate it hungrily, but here the civility ended. Afterwards, they were marched to a cell and locked in. The puddle on the floor and the unmistakable smell left them in no doubt that in the next one was an overflowing toilet, yet their shouts and hammering on the door came to nothing, and exhausted they fell asleep on the filthy floor.

The next day, the Italians meant business. With hands and later also feet tied, the trio were marched to the shore and placed in a caique for return to Kythnos. Here, half the garrison were waiting, and they were not pleased to see these men who had humiliated them. As a transport lorry pulled up, Natusch lashed out at an Italian who had just cuffed him around the ear, and earned a severe beating for his trouble. On the road to the island headquarters, six men rode in the lorry with them armed with revolvers. The Italians were taking no chances. The Kythnos commandante however was a very different man from his counterpart on Kea. He took them to his office, got medical attention for the cut on Natusch's head received during the beating, and gave Macaskie his first cigarette in days. The commandante was a humane man, but explained that he was to hold them for just one night before they were to be handed on to Syros, the headquarters of the

Italian Aegean Command, for further questioning. After Rhodes, Syros boasted the largest garrison in the region, and when they got there they were met by an escort of black shirted carabinieri. The authorities here were not sure what to make of these Allied prisoners. Only garbled accounts had come from the other garrisons, but after a couple of hours of questioning by the area commander, Colonel Giovanni Duca, they were no further on. Just to be on the safe side, Syros HQ also classified them as spies, but for good measure added the additional charge of war crimes.

The first night they were thrown into an overcrowded cell, filled with Greeks – mostly black market types or thieves. The main piece of information which they managed to obtain about this place was that the food was bad, and so it proved, to begin with at least. After nine days an officer informed them that they were being moved – the spying and war crimes charges were to be dropped, and they would now be granted PoW status. This came with extra food and five cigarettes apiece. That afternoon they were moved to better accommodation, with army beds, three blankets each, two hours' exercise a day instead of the five minutes accorded the criminals, and best of all, full army rations. Macaskie being an officer received more, but the three pooled everything they had. Other advantages included access to a barber and bathing facilities. Their clothes, full of lice and fleas from the civilian jail, were put through a steam press. The only downside to their new quarters was that unlike the criminal cell, which had offered possibilities for a break out had they remained there, this place was escape-proof. The walls were solid and over four feet thick. The windows were barred, and sentries patrolled day and night. They were to spend the next three months here, without the remotest possibility of getting away.

During that time the Italians had been investigating Macaskie's movements, and at last they had a breakthrough. It appears that they managed to find someone in Athens who knew him, and was prepared to talk. The informer did not know enough to get him condemned out of hand, but what he did say gave the Contra Spionaggio, who had been suspicious from the outset, confidence that they were on the right track and motivation to carry on searching for the missing pieces of the puzzle. In the meantime, they sent word to have Frank placed in solitary confinement. The rest of the trio were moved to another cell, with orders not to speak to him, or attempt any form of communication. They exercised at different times now, and the only time the others saw him was at his window, but they still kept in touch. Macaskie had had a presentiment that something like this might happen, and had devised a simple system for that eventuality. They wrote messages to each other and hid them on the lintel above the lavatory door. Frank collected his messages on his visit, and in turn left replies and requests. Jones left him his daily ration of four cigarettes each day and this, along with the fact that his cell was large and airy, with two large windows that gave a good view of everything going on outside, undoubtedly contributed to keeping up his morale.

This period lasted for the whole of March 1942, and at Easter that year the Italian garrison held a bigger celebration than usual. Singapore had fallen not long before, and they were jubilant. The Axis star was at its zenith, and many among them gave the war six months before a successful conclusion. The prisoners were allowed to attend Easter Mass, and Macaskie managed to speak to the others informing them that he was due to be tried as a spy. They were downcast, but he urged them not to worry, because as he put it there was life in the old dog yet. After Mass, the most extraordinary event occurred. About mid-day a procession toured the camp, led by the head cook with his bevy of kitchen staff behind him. At each cell he stopped, and as the doors were opened and dixies offered up, they were filled first with minestrone soup, followed by pasta asciutta. A third lackey carried rosy apples and a fourth poured out Chianti. A fifth meanwhile offered nuts and figs. The showpiece however was left to the head cook. Taking a dish from one of his retainers he offered each man a freshly made piping-hot hot cross bun. As he basked in the gratitude of the prisoners, he bowed and wished them Buon Appetito.

A week later they were leaving Syros. All of the original Piraeus party now met again in the hold of a tramp steamer. Georgios Trypanis, Alexis Lados and the others had been kept in a civilian prison not far away, where they had learned that their destination was Rhodes. Like Frank, Lados and Chrysinis were to face espionage charges. The elder of the two Georgios was also in serious trouble. He was now charged with assisting an enemy agent (ie Macaskie) and if he was found guilty, Georgios would automatically suffer the same fate. The two men conversed in low voices. It seemed that the Italians had dug up more evidence against them. In fact, when Macaskie, the Liverpudlian and the New Zealander were captured at Kea and taken captive to Syros, the Italian counterintelligence service had sent a signal to Smyrna, asking about the British officer. It was now that Macaskie was to pay dearly for one of his most reckless actions: before leaving there for Greece, and despite Noël Rees's advice to stay hidden, he was determined to visit the beautiful lady who he said he would later marry. At her home, however, he ran into the wife of Rudolf de Zandonati, a wealthy resident of Bornova and also one of the twenty-five or so secret informants of the Italian espionage service in Smyrna. De Zandonati, when contacted, confirmed the details of Macaskie's stay in Smyrna, so his cover story, that he was left in Greece with the departure of the British, was undermined. From here on he and Ladas were considered by the Italians to be spies, and Chrysinis an accomplice. Macaskie it seems was never to learn of the betrayal of Adosidou, who was another of his lovers. For reasons that are not clear, the decision to keep the information from him was taken by Rees, in spite of his anger towards her. However, the proposal to award her a medal after the liberation of Greece would be blocked by British intelligence.

George also knew that the resistance had found the informer in Athens and liquidated him, but the damage was already done and this would not help their prospects now. What they did not know, however was that by this time the Greek underground grapevine had informed British intelligence in Cairo of the situation Frank, Alexis and Chrysinis were in. Unbeknown to the trio, a rescue plan had been formulated to position a submarine just off the island of Samos, in order to intercept and torpedo the vessel carrying the party south. Another MI9 officer, Captain Michael Woodbine-Parish MC

DSM (Greece) and his crew of latter day 'pirates' (who were at that point touring the Aegean islands in a caique, looking for British and Commonwealth fugitives) would then be ordered to rendezvous, and pick up the survivors from the sinking vessel. Fortuitously for the Macaskie party, at the last minute the submarine was ordered to another mission. Given the effect of a submarine attack on merchant shipping, particularly one carrying prisoners below the waterline, the collateral damage done may well have killed the entire group that they were intending to save. What the three men did know was that the forthcoming trial was likely to be a farce, and that their best chance of survival lay in escape.

It was Natusch who now came up with the plan. The only exit from the hold was up a vertical 30-foot ladder which was guarded at the bottom by six Italians. Three hundred soldiers were billeted aft of the bridge, so no sentries had been detailed to guard the top of the ladder. The prisoners were allowed up once a day to visit the lavatory on the deck, which was how they had ascertained this information. At 3am one of the prisoners, an amateur boxer, was to ask one of the sentries for a light, before laying him out with a punch. At this point, others would overpower the rest, taking their rifles. Armed with these, the prisoners would then climb the ladder and rush the bridge from both sides. The Breda machine guns on the bridge would then be reversed and used to keep the rest of the Italians in check, which would be easy as there were only two doors giving access to the deck from their quarters. The ship would then be turned towards the Turkish coast where it would be beached. Despite a number of obvious snags in the scheme, the others agreed to go along with it, and it was decided to strike as soon as the ship entered the straits between Rhodes and Turkey. This stretch of water was only 15 miles wide, so they reasoned that if the ship went down the middle, they would only be some 7 or 8 miles from the Turkish shore.

No one could be certain about the currents which might be running in that channel, but neither Macaskie nor George worried about this. In the water there was a chance. In an Italian jail there was none. If the ship could be beached, then every man would be for himself, but if it could not, then these two were going over the side. Slowly the days went by, until the ship called at the last island halt before Rhodes. Here, the jinx which had dogged Macaskie since leaving Athens visited them again. At this island a party of infantry boarded the steamer. As all the accommodation had been allocated, these men were forced to sleep on the deck. About fifty of them stretched out their blankets on the hatch above the prisoners, who could clearly hear them cursing about the cold. Even Natusch was now forced to admit that the plan was hopeless. The steamer went on to Rhodes, where the party split up. Most of the British and Commonwealth prisoners went on to a ship bound for the Italian PoW reception centre at Bari. Macaskie and the Greeks remained on Rhodes, destined for trial. When the truck transporting them arrived at the Kaskinou Prison, the chief warden, Signor Periano was at the gate waiting to meet them. With his plump rosy face and cheery smile he looked for all the world like a suave hotel manager welcoming his guests. 'Benvenuti a la Villa Marina,' he called out.

With their typical black humour the Italians had christened the jail thus because of its close proximity to the sea. Periano was enormously proud of his prison, and fussy about it. He took himself very seriously and at first was quite high-handed towards the escapers, but at heart he was a kindly man and eventually came to respect the group he now baptised in a humorous manner the 'Familia Reale.' They were after all a cut above most of his run of the mill prisoners, consisting of two Oxbridge men (Macaskie and Trypanis), two Athens College graduates (Ladas and Paspatis), and one high-ranking civil servant.

Macaskie was under no illusion that the planned court room proceedings were anything but a sham, and the Italians fully intended to shoot him, it was just a question of when. After three weeks of confinement on Rhodes he and the Greeks destined to be tried with him decided to make a break. It was Alexis who came up with the plan. He noticed that at meal times, when all the prisoners were congregating to receive their ration, the guards sometimes positioned the large steaming vat of soup in a place where they could not easily see the whole compound. In this circumstance, if others shielded them from view those who were served first might be able to slip unnoticed into the prison's outer courtyard and there scale the wall. If they were noticed and an alarm sounded, they could simply state that they had wandered away to eat their meal in the sunshine. They might be knocked about a little by the guards and end up in a punishment cell, but it would not look like an escape attempt. If on the other hand they were not observed, they could get away by climbing the prison wall, using a number of nearby benches stacked one atop another. Another prisoner had given them an address of someone in the town, which was about 8 kilometres away, who would help them onto a boat for Turkey.

It was decided that Frank and Alexis would make the attempt, as these were most at risk from the firing squad, and also they were the fittest, the rest being severely weakened by malnutrition caused by the starvation rations. For days they made sure they were always at the front of the food queue, to the annoyance of the other prisoners who thought they wanted the oil which usually floated to the top of the soup. Then at last, one day their chance came. Having taken their bowl and bread, the two casually wandered off down the passage, whilst the rest of the group returned to the cells. Ordinarily, given an hour's grace to get away, they could have hidden on a large island like Rhodes indefinitely. Instead, an informer within the prison gave them away to the Italians after just ten minutes; this man, who had only been there a few days, and was a stool pigeon, was watching furtively. He seemed puzzled, and after a while he knocked on the cell door. He whispered something to the guard and was let out. Suddenly there were angry voices outside and the door burst open, Periano and two guards strode in. The prisoners tried to spread out to cover the gaps in their ranks as best they could. The warden's face was a mixture of anger and confusion. He knew something was going on but could not quite make out just what. At last he decided to count them, and it was then finally that the penny dropped. Paspatis continues:

> The Capo screamed as shrilly as an elephant and stood staring round at us, his little piggy eyes reddening slowly. Then he lost his head and striding up and down the middle of the cell cursed God and the Virgin and all of us for being born. At last it dropped. 'L'inglese!' he shouted, rushing down at us. 'Dov'e l'Inglese?' Suddenly he lost his fierce expression and was pleading with us. 'Where is he? Where is he?' Our faces registered blank stupidity. Where indeed? I looked under Frank's bed with apparent earnestness. 'Pig!' he screamed, clutching me by the collar. 'You think it's funny! I'll show you how funny it is later. And who's the other one?' At last he had managed to count up to two again.
>
> 'Who?' we all echoed unhelpfully. I could almost begin to feel sorry for him. He looked as if on the point of having a stroke and every minute he wasted was a minute gained for Frank and Alexis. 'The lavatory?' Philip suggested. The little door nearly fell to pieces as the Capo kicked it open. Someone unwisely giggled. 'Signor Peranio,' said one of the guards, 'the other is the tall, thin one, Ladas.' 'Where are they?' the Capo shouted in my face, so close he was covering me with a shower of spit. 'You know where they are, you dirty lying bastards. You're helping your spy friends.'[4]

In fact they had made it no further than the ditch outside the prison, and here they were recaptured. What neither had accounted for was how much their bodies had been weakened by malnutrition, and having scaled the wall they collapsed exhausted, unable to go any further. It is possible that Macaskie, who had not been subjected to the same starvation diet during his first months of captivity, could have gone on, but chose not to abandon Ladas who was in poor shape. Thrown into the punishment cells, Frank expected the worst when he was called before General Rino Rossi, the President of the Italian Military Court on Rhodes. He foresaw severe punishment, but instead found that the general was a holder of the British Military Cross from the First World War, which he evidently felt to be a great honour. He had been a prisoner of war – and an escaper – himself, and so in him Macaskie found something of a kindred spirit. Frank recounted his meeting with him in warm terms:

> I expected all kinds of horrible punishments for what I had done but I discovered to my amazement that the General was a violent Anglophile … It was obvious that General Rossi was more interested in my story to compare methods of escape employed, than in the administration of justice. The General almost went so far as to infer that I had only done my duty. As a result of this, Alexis, the skipper and myself received far better treatment. General Rossi, by various ruses, postponed our trial, and one day he came to see me and proudly showed me his MC.[5]

Rossi was also a Philhellene, and hated fascists and Nazis. After the war, he would be honoured with a Greek medal.

The escape attempt had caused official embarrassment and in his report on the matter, Rossi put the blame on the harsh regime at the Villa Marina. He ensured that living conditions improved and there was no further mistreatment, the prisoners even being taken down to the beach and allowed to swim, but security was tightened and there was no other opportunity to escape on Rhodes. Rossi had wanted to try the men in his own jurisdiction, but the Military Court was eventually set up on Samos, and so a strong escort was to take the prisoners there. They were loaded aboard the steamer *Fiume*, carrying supplies to the Italian troops on that island. British submarines were active in these waters, and the captain was aware of the risks to his ship. In order to try to protect it, he had the captives chained to a bench on the upper deck, believing that no British captain would attack if he saw prisoners on board. It was in reality only good fortune that spared the ship this time, for the prisoners would hardly have been visible through a periscope at wavetop height, and she was indeed to be sunk shortly afterwards. On 23 May 1942, the prisoners arrived on Samos; Macaskie, Ladas and Chrysinis went to the prison in Vathi, the rest were set free under surveillance. Those in Vathi were no longer under the watchful eye of the general, and so the unpalatable diet of boiled maize resumed once more.

The basis of the charge against Macaskie was that he had been caught in civilian clothes, without a uniform, and so in order to muddy the waters Georgios Paspatis suggested that he provide him with one. Macaskie wondered how this could be possible, but at this point Paspatis was free to move about during the day, and only locked in cells at night, so he went around among the many prisoners held there trying to find military clothes, and to barter for them. Soon he found a pair of army trousers which he was able to secure. This was followed before long by an old uniform shirt. To Macaskie the flaw in the plan lay in rank insignia. Where would they find six metal pips for a captain in an Italian prison? George answered that he should say that, although he was captured in winter, he was still wearing his summer uniform underneath civilian clothes, for warmth. Summer uniforms did not necessarily have metal pips, indeed it was quite usual to find cloth ones. George suggested embroidering some and slipping them over the epaulettes of the shirt, as was common practice in the British Army. He volunteered to try to undertake the embroidery, despite the fact that Macaskie had never bothered to pay much attention to rank pips, and could not describe them.

Paspatis just had to improvise as best he could from his own memory, but by using some brown and white threads from a rag and, working unobserved whenever he could, with a precious needle which he had been lucky enough to find hidden by another prisoner, the results were quite convincing. However he had only finished five of the six needed when Macaskie was summoned by the Italians for his next interrogation. Thinking quickly, he tore that part of the epaulette to make it seem as if it had been ripped off. In fact, so impressive did Macaskie appear in his new uniform, that as he walked out of his cell the Italian soldiers were taken by surprise, and they stood to attention and saluted. The fact that he was in uniform during the interrogation appeared to undermine the original accusation that he had been in civilian clothes when captured, and was

Greece and the Aegean Sea, showing locations mentioned in the text. (Author's Copyright)

Frank Macaskie as a Prefect at Warwick School, seated next to headmaster Riding. (Courtesy of Gervald Frykman)

Above: A school rugby cap from 1928, won by Macaskie at Warwick School. (Courtesy of Macaskie family)

Left: Aideen Riding, the wife of Macaskie's headmaster, and object of his schoolboy affection. (Courtesy of Gervald Frykman)

Frank Macaskie and his brother John on holiday in the 1930s. (Courtesy of Macaskie family)

Frank Macaskie at Oxford University. (Courtesy of Macaskie family)

Italian prisoners captured in the Western Desert enter a POW cage, early 1941. (Library of Congress)

Above left: Private John Lippett, a battalion cook, who was preparing breakfast on Crete on the first morning when the Luftwaffe attacked. (Author's Collection)

Above right: Captain John Marriott MC, battalion adjutant of the 2nd Leicesters. (Author's Collection)

German paratroopers landing on Crete, May 1941. (Author's Collection)

Above left: Private Stan Seddon, who fought alongside Macaskie at the airfield on Crete in May 1941. (Author's collection)

Above right: A rare photo of 2nd Leicesters mortarman, Private Jack Barker taken on Crete, illustrating the kit that was carried and uniform that was worn. (Author's Collection)

Right: German paratroopers in action on Crete, May 1941. (Public Domain)

Above left: Lela Karagianni, who assisted Macaskie in his first escape from enemy captivity. She was executed by the Germans shortly before Athens was liberated. (Public Domain)

Above right: Macaskie in khaki drill uniform, with rank of lieutenant. This photo was probably taken in Cairo following his first escape from Greece, and before the award of the Military Cross. (Courtesy of Macaskie family)

Lieutenant Colonel Tony Simonds, Macaskie's superior at N Section, 'A' Force. (Courtesy of Rosey Woollcombe)

PASSPORT.

By His Majesty's

CONSUL - GENERAL

at

CAIRO.

These are to request and require in the Name of His Majesty all those whom it may concern to allow the bearer to pass freely without let or hindrance and to afford him or her every assistance and protection of which he or she may stand in need.

Given at

CAIRO.

the 20TH day

of OCTOBER 1941.

H.M. CONSUL.

for H.M. CONSUL GENERAL.

1

This Passport contains 32 pages.

Ce passeport contient 32 pages.

PASSPORT.

PASSEPORT.

UNITED KINGDOM OF GREAT BRITAIN AND NORTHERN IRELAND.

ROYAUME-UNI DE GRANDE-BRETAGNE ET D'IRLANDE DU NORD.

No. of PASSPORT / No. du PASSEPORT: C. 156090

NAME OF BEARER / NOM DU TITULAIRE: MR. JOHN MACASKIE.

ACCOMPANIED BY HIS WIFE (Maiden name) / ACCOMPAGNÉ DE SA FEMME (Née)

and by / et de ... children / enfants

NATIONAL STATUS / NATIONALITÉ

BRITISH SUBJECT BY BIRTH.

The false passport with which Macaskie was provided, in order to cross into and out of Turkey. (Courtesy of Macaskie family)

Above left: Aggelos Evert the Athens police chief, who assisted British escapers, and Jews facing persecution, with fake documents. (Public Domain)

Above middle: Alexis Ladas, of the Royal Hellenic Airforce, who went to Athens as Macaskie's interpreter, and later stood trial with him. (Public Domain)

Above right: A portrait sketch of Francis Jones, from the frontispiece of *Escape to Nowhere*. (Courtesy of Hugh Hassard Jones)

Above left: Bill Natusch, the New Zealander who was captured with Jones and Macaskie on Kea. (Public Domain)

Above right: Besi Adosidou, who betrayed Macaskie to the Italians on Syros. (Public Domain)

Left: Colonel Giovanni Duca, Italian commander of Syros. Later in the war, after the Italian armistice he became a resistance leader himself and was killed by the SS in 1944. (Public Domain)

Above left: Rino Rossi, Italian commander on Rhodes. He forged a friendship with Macaskie, and tried to assist him. (Public Domain)

Above middle: Irenios Papamichael, Bishop of Samos. He opposed the actions of the Italian authorities and strove to protect the island's people during the occupation. He also assisted Macaskie. (Public Domain)

Above right: General Carlo Vecchiarelli, Italian commander in Athens, 1943. (Public Domain)

Macaskie (back row centre) outside the condemned cell in Kallithea prison. The photo was smuggled out by Commander Vernicos. (Michael Woodbine Parish. Courtesy of Robin Woodbine Parish)

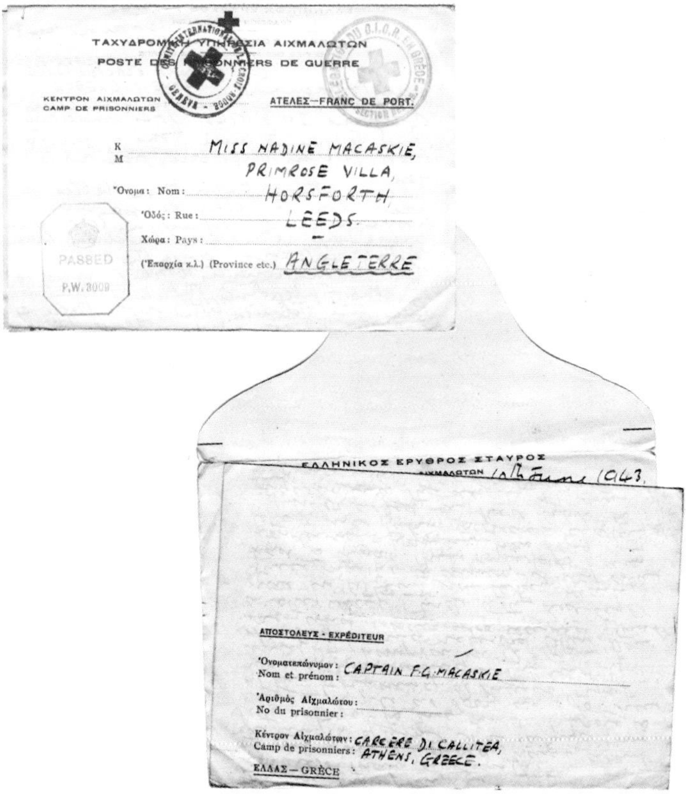

POW letters sent by Macaskie via the Red Cross in June 1943. (Courtesy of Macaskie family)

Averoff Prison, after the liberation of Athens. (Public Domain)

Above left: Nicholas Hammond, SOE officer and commander of the Allied Military Mission to Greece. (Public Domain)

Above right: Macaskie wearing the beard that he grew in 1944 as part of his disguise as 'Major Parkes'. (Courtesy of Macaskie family)

Above left: Macaskie's nemesis, ELAS leader Andreas Mountrichas, known as 'Orestis'. Although he rose through the communist hierarchy, he was later denounced by his former comrades as an 'enemy agent' because he came to terms with the establishment. (Public Domain)

Above right: General Hellmuth Felmy, German commander in southern Greece. He was convicted of war crimes at Nuremberg, but his sentence was reduced on appeal. (Public Domain)

Crowds celebrate on liberation day, Athens 11 October 1944. (Public Domain)

Macaskie with Brigadier George Jellicoe (left) and Shan Sedgwick (right), on the day of liberation in Athens. 11 October 1944. (Copyright Mary Henderson, reproduced from *Xenia A Memoir*)

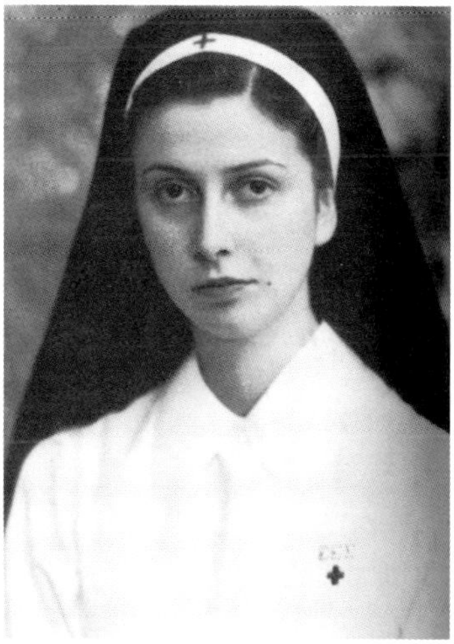

Above left: John Redpath DCM, the New Zealander who served in MI9 alongside Macaskie in 1944 and 1945. (Public Domain)

Above right: Mary Cawadias, the Greek nurse who was Macaskie's girlfriend from 1944 to 1945. (Copyright Mary Henderson, reproduced from *Xenia A Memoir*)

Right: Georgios Seferiades (Seferis), the Nobel prize winner who worked closely with Macaskie in the early postwar years. (Public Domain)

Archbishop Damaskinos aboard HMS *Ajax*, Christmas Day 1944. Frank Macaskie stands to the left. This was the occasion of the Archbishop's meeting with Winston Churchill. (Courtesy of Macaskie family)

Macaskie and Archbishop Damaskinos. Macaskie wears ribbons of the MC and bar, Africa Star and 1939-45 Star, and rank of Major, suggesting a date around May 1945. (Courtesy of Macaskie family)

Damaskinos at a meal with British prime minister Clement Attlee, 10 September 1945. Macaskie seated on the right. (Courtesy of Macaskie family)

Damaskinos meets the Archbishop of Canterbury, September 1945. Macaskie extreme left. (Courtesy of Macaskie family)

Above: George Polk, the American journalist murdered in Athens during the Greek civil war. (Public Domain)

Right: Macaskie in Greece with journalist Mario Modiano, around 1947. (Centropa Archive)

Above left: Cyrus Leo Sulzberger, the American journalist (and possible CIA asset) who knew Macaskie in post-war Greece. (Public Domain)

Above right: King Paul of Greece, who inherited the throne from his brother George in 1947. (Public Domain)

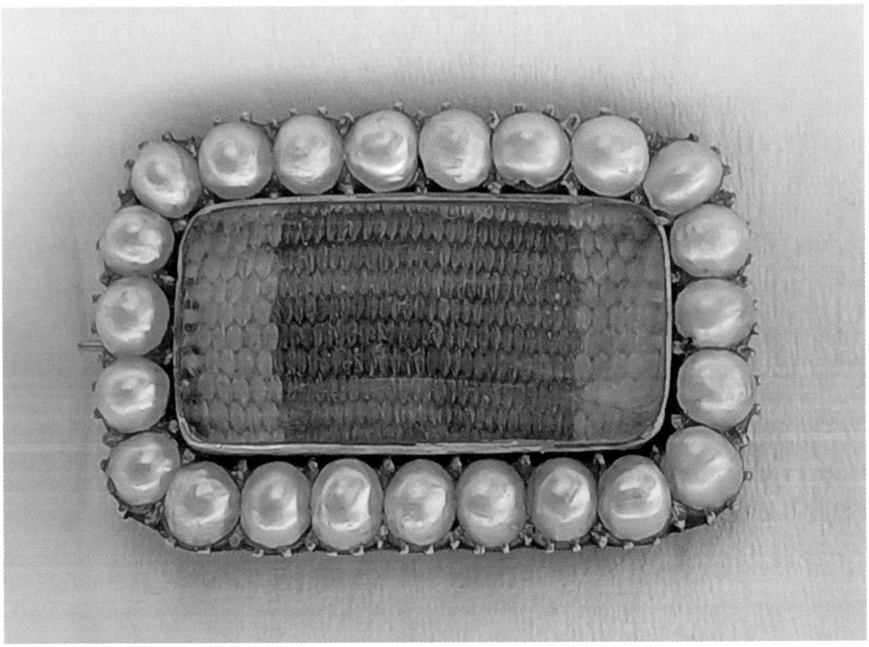

A gold and pearl brooch incorporating a piece of Military Cross ribbon, probably given by Frank to one of his sisters just after the war. (Courtesy of Macaskie family)

therefore a spy. His story about the summer uniform, and having been given clothes to wear over it by a shepherd went down well, and the whole thing caused a much-needed delay whilst the military court on Samos sought further clarification.

It was obvious to all that the Italians had mixed feelings about the British, and even though Macaskie was now their prisoner they were still somewhat in awe of him. It turned out that one of the Italian guards was a featherweight boxing champion, and the authorities came up with an idea of teaching the Englishman a lesson. They thought that if challenged he would surely take on the smaller Italian, not knowing he was a champion, and would receive a sound thrashing which would bring him down a peg or two in the eyes of the rest of the guards. Indeed, given Frank's poor physical shape by this point, it was pretty much a certainty. So the prison commander announced that to entertain the prisoners, a boxing match would be held in the courtyard between an ordinary Italian soldier, and a British officer. For his part, Macaskie was not the sort of man to refuse a challenge, even if he was not in the best physical condition.

The next day, all of the prisoners and most of the guards gathered around a temporary ring in in the courtyard, and the match began. The first round went badly for Frank. The fast and agile featherweight ran rings around him, and Macaskie, stiff and out of practice, was jabbed and punched repeatedly. When the second round started, the Italian came on as before, jabbing Frank hard in the face and landing a blow which made him reel. As the Italian came rushing in to finish him off, something entirely unexpected happened. It happened almost too quickly to see, but there was a crash and the cocky featherweight was lifted bodily into the air before coming down in a heap, arms and legs everywhere. For a fraction of a second there was silence, then a tremendous roaring cheer filled the prison courtyard and spilled over the walls. His fellow prisoners knew then that Frank would not go down that easily. Now, one could make out on his face an unusual and quite frightening expression of anger. For his part, the Italian was quickly back on his feet and was closing in again, raining blows once more. Something was different now though; he was still attacking, but Frank's punch must have unsettled him because he was notably less cocky and more wary. Macaskie's mood had also changed. He was finding his feet now and as well as parrying most of the punches, for a second time he struck out. This time it happened slowly enough for all to see, a magnificently timed left hook, followed by an uppercut. The little Italian's head shook from side to side and he went sprawling. The referee ended the round a little too early it seemed, and the Italian guards were now a sea of gloomy faces. The prisoners, by contrast, were jubilant. Round three came, and with it a resurgent Frank. Instead of tiring from the effort thus far, he seemed to be drawing on some unseen source of energy. No longer on the back foot, he landed blow after blow, driving his opponent across the ring. When the little Italian went down again, the referee was so stunned that he forgot to begin the count. One of the prisoners jumped into the ring and began it for him, but he only got as far as six. The featherweight got to his feet, but instead of returning to the bout stumbled off out of the ring. The prison authorities had reckoned without Macaskie's boxing experience both at public school and at Oxford. The match had done much to raise the spirits of the prisoners as a whole, but for the Macaskie party there was still the lingering threat of execution.

Death was growing ever closer and so Frank, Alexis and Chrysinis found another opportunity to escape, this time by forcing the bars on the cell window with a piece of iron from the frame of a bed, whilst other prisoners drowned out the noise by singing. They had a rough ladder, made from wood and nails from the same bed, and together they climbed onto the prison roof, pulling the ladder up behind them. In theory it should have been easy for them to drop down into the street, reach the eastern end of the island and swim or row the four miles to Turkey, but once again, fate intervened. A group of Italian soldiers were sleeping on the ground below. Alexis wanted to wait until the guards at the other end of the building had started their circuit, but Macaskie favoured the more direct route, and so they decided to go their own separate ways. Macaskie got down without waking the guards, and got away, but the others were recaptured. When he reached a pre-arranged rendezvous point, he found the Italians already waiting for him. Back in prison once more, security was tightened even further. As punishment for their escape attempt, they were beaten up by the guards and henceforth were locked in the basement of the prison, in isolation. The guards now remained in the cells to keep a closer eye on the trio. Living conditions deteriorated even more, as sewer rats and other vermin tormented them. However for others in the party not under close arrest there was unexpected news. In July, Georgios Paspatis received a visit from a barber, with a message sent by Noël Rees. On such a day, at such a time, he must be in a grove of trees somewhere on the island, where he would be met by a guide. Paspatis announced the plan to the rest of the group, but the others, with the exception of Messinezis, hesitated. Thus, on 18 July Paspatis and Messinezis alone fled to Turkey.

Back in Cairo, efforts continued to find a way of extricating Macaskie; Captain Michael Woodbine Parish, his fellow MI9 officer who was at large in the Greek islands with a raiding party, was their liaison. In September 1942 he proposed a scheme whereby his local contacts would create a diversion, the destruction of six vessels in construction in one harbour and a seventh in another, to be set on fire by means of cotton waste soaked in petrol. Whilst the authorities were dealing with this, it was envisaged that Macaskie would escape from prison and either rendezvous with a boat sent to pick him up, or failing this, swim to the Turkish mainland. For a strong swimmer like Macaskie this should be possible as it was only twenty minutes to an island in the channel and a further ten minutes from there to the coast of Turkey. However this was not as easy as it might at first appear.

The prison commandant, who the trio referred to as 'the Dog', was an overbearing bully who regarded Macaskie as the most prized butterfly that he had in his collection – a beautiful and rare specimen; an English officer no less. By the same token the two Greeks were ugly moths, drab and uninteresting, the underlings of a conquered nation. Frank's calmness, poise and dignity impressed his thuggish host. Equally compelling was his immaculate appearance. Macaskie slept with his trousers under the mattress each night so that the crease would be freshly pressed each morning. He immediately removed any stains or mud from his trousers and shoes, and washed his white shirt daily. This English captain was too important a prize for the commandant to lose, but at the same time he liked to taunt him. One day he announced that, as the British were so fond of exercise, a special compound was to be built for the three, to be known as the 'drawing room.' However the 'drawing room' turned out to be a concrete box with hardly enough room to move in, and the only light coming from a small slit of a window high up near the ceiling, behind bars. Besy Adosidou was Macaskie's only officially allowed contact with the outside world here, and it was through her that messages were passed back and forth between him and Woodbine Parish. The latter now favoured either breaking into the gaol, or setting off bombs in the neighbourhood of the prison, in Italian stores or other facilities, creating a diversion for a breakout. For this purpose Woodbine Parish requested fifteen to twenty incendiary bombs be dispatched to him by Cairo. Macaskie had asked for plans and information on the attitude of the guards to be supplied, as well as guides made available to conduct him to a boat, in the event of a successful escape. He did not however approve of the bombs, possibly because of the risk of civilian casualties. It seems that Besy had not fled to Smyrna with Paspatis when she had the chance, because the rumour that she had betrayed the group was in widespread circulation there, and she feared repercussions. However, Woodbine Parish reported that she was now asking for transport to Turkey to be arranged for her. He was concerned by this, as she was his only means of communication with Macaskie. He added in his report:

> Mrs Baum [Besy] I understand is a lady of considerable charm and attraction. This, according to our agent on the spot, was well noted by Courvoissier the head of the Red Cross. In fact he recently called at this office and told us that Mrs Baum wanted to come over at the earliest available opportunity to discuss matters with us here. This has created rather a problem because although she will no doubt have interesting views on Felix's [Macaskie's] future and ideas on how he may effect his escape, her coming over will mean we will lose our contact with Felix.[6]

He advised that once she had left, she could not go back, and suggested that she should be asked to remain for at least another month. Concern for Frank was now also growing at MI9 headquarters in London, and in October, Brigadier Crockatt and Lieutenant Colonel Clarke met to discuss his case with Major General Ernest Gepp (Director of the Prisoners of War Office), and to go over their options. It was decided not to contest the allegation that he was in civilian clothes, but to stress that he was merely attempting to rescue Allied prisoners. However, one of the instructions which came from this meeting was to 'Make absolutely certain of [the] complete truth. Have you definite proof Macaskie had no wireless and was not in any way involved in other more sinister activity?'[7]

Simonds responded to Crockatt's request for clarification on this by asserting that Macaskie had no wireless, no instructions to deal in espionage and carried no papers. Whether Rees had unofficially encouraged him to exceed his brief is not certain, but it would seem clear that some of Macaskie's actions in contacting resistance and political leaders in Athens had indeed gone beyond merely assisting evaders. In the meantime, a letter written by Frank to his mother in November turned up in Leeds some months later, having passed through Italian censorship. Extracts were forwarded to Simonds for information:

> I am allowed to write to you again, but there is little I can tell you … I am still in prison on the island of Samos awaiting court-martial in the hands of the Italians. I keep very fit but the boredom of life is indescribable. I am in a cell with two other people – both Greeks, but fortunately one of them can speak English perfectly … I haven't seen an Englishman for nearly a year now … I am afraid it is still no good your writing to me. If I had known I was going to be in Rhodes and here all this time I wouldn't have said this before, but I can't be kept here much longer and I hope soon to be able to give you a permanent address to write to and to be able to write to you regularly … Don't worry about me. I feel confident I shall survive the court-martial … I will write to you whenever I am allowed and you may be sure that I always will.[8]

The two Greek prisoners were tired now and hoping for a rest from escape attempts, but Macaskie was angry and immediately began planning how they could get out of the 'drawing room'. They kept up their spirits by singing songs like *Carry me back to Old Virginny* at the top of their voices, teaching Chrysinis English poetry, and by Frank reciting the ancient Greek eulogy of the 300 Spartans who were killed at the Battle of Thermopylae. Gradually a plan was hatched. They could not tunnel out because the walls were too thick, but the bars at the window could be cut if they could somehow get their hands on a hacksaw or file. At this point however, they found an unexpected ally. Irenios, the Bishop of Samos, was a staunch patriot. Relations between him and the Italian authorities were never good, but when Genetto Bianco was appointed governor on the island, and sought to turn the people towards Fascism, Irenios delivered thunderbolt after thunderbolt at him from his pulpit. A Greek text records that not only were the escapers living in terrible conditions in prison, but also many Samians, overcrowded, sick, ragged and unhappy. Red Cross supplies were controlled by Bianco's wife, and so their only hope was the church. The commandant allowed a young girl on the Bishop's staff, Danai Synanidou, into the prison to bring them food. Clothed in a simple black dress and with head covered in a black scarf she appeared to be just an ordinary Greek woman, but she was as dedicated as any to the cause of Greece and one day whispered to Alexis that she wished to help them. Ladas immediately remembered the blade that they needed, but was at a loss to work out how she could bring it in. All the food that she brought to them was carefully scrutinised, and even the bread was cut up into small chunks to prevent anything being sent in inside it.

Nonetheless it was Ladas who came up with the plan. He realised that if Macaskie's shoes wore out, the commandant would have to ask Danai to acquire some new ones for him, and the blade could be smuggled in inside these. Having told Danai of the scheme, he came to Frank to discuss it with him, but Macaskie was reluctant to part with his carefully kept shoes. In the end he did agree, and joined the others in damaging them deliberately. The next morning at exercise time, the guards were amazed to see the normally immaculately turned out Macaskie marching around the muddy courtyard barefoot – though otherwise fully of his usual poise and bearing. The matter soon reached the commandant and, livid, he summoned Alexis for an explanation and to vent his wrath. Although Ladas feared another beating, he cooly explained to 'the Dog' that Macaskie's shoes had simply worn out. He added that a British captain should not be walking around barefoot, and that it was the commandant's duty to provide a new pair, invoking the Geneva Convention for good measure.

He mentioned that Danai might be able to supply some shoes at no cost to him, to which the commandant unexpectedly agreed. When he learned that the plan was going ahead, Macaskie began to work out the details, and asked Alexis how they could take Danai with them. He replied that they could not, as she had a crippled mother for whom she had to care. At this point Frank announced that the whole thing was off, as he would not leave the girl to face her fate – and the wrath of 'the Dog' when he found out – alone. The others knew that there was no point trying to persuade him, as he had made up his mind. There was however a sequel to this incident, and one in which the escapers could make use of Danai's willingness to help, without placing her in immediate danger:

During this time, the British secret service, which was based in Smyrna, sent a message to Irenios, with a fervent request to do everything possible for their salvation. At the risk of his life, he visited each, doing what he could to help. Unfortunately, his actions were of no use, as the Italians had decided to send the three men to Italy to be executed as spies. With no other option, the bishop urgently contacted Major P. Paraschakis.

'I want you to find me a reliable shoemaker,' he told him. 'Can you?'

'I can,' he answered in surprise, 'But I do not understand why?'

'You will understand, when I tell you that the heels of the shoes must have special compartments.'

'So?'

'So that in each heel can be hidden at least £10.'

Thus he explained to him that Frank Macaskie and his two Greek companions had to take money with them. Perhaps in this way they would manage to buy off one of their guards to help them escape. The shoes were taken to the prison by a daring girl, Danai Synanidou who, oblivious to the dangers, maintained a secret correspondence with the prisoners.[9]

On Christmas Day the delighted commandant produced the shoes with all the pomp and ceremony that he could muster. They were not Macaskie's usual style of footwear, indeed the high black shiny boots were perhaps originally the Bishop's own personal property. After the presentation, Frank asked the commandant if he might see the girl – who he had not yet met – and thank her personally. Up to now, her only contact had been with Alexis, but she longed to meet the heroic British captain. Under the supervision of the guards, a brief meeting was permitted. To the church chronicle account above can be added the fact that Irenios managed to appoint a Greek as their jailer, but the keys were in the hands of an Italian who was waiting to receive his pension and was reluctant to help. Just before Christmas, Simonds prepared a report on a number of 'A' Force personnel who had been captured by the Italians. For Macaskie, he noted that communication was extremely difficult as he was not being held as a PoW. Although letters of encouragement would greatly aid his morale, any attempt at communication via the Red Cross should emanate from London, rather than Cairo, lest it should fuel suspicions that the Italians already had that he had been sent on a secret mission from Egypt. He included a paragraph from Rees which stated:

> Our friend in prison is being well looked after by our organisation, especially by our Bishop who in a proper way recommended Mrs 'Commissario' to intervene on his behalf that he should be considered as a prisoner of war, alleging that he was arrested with his uniform on,

> and suggesting that he should be exchanged if possible against one of her own sons now a prisoner of war in the hands of the Rams [codeword for Americans].[10]

The identity of Mrs 'Commissario' is not clear but she might well have been the wife of Genetto Bianco. Simonds added that it was known that Macaskie was desperately short of food, medical supplies and warm clothes. His condition was thought to be very bad, and lacking almost everything necessary for survival. He had been taught PoW code No2, and allotted a frequency, though it was probable he had forgotten it. As well as the lack of food, the six or seven months spent in isolation here dragged even more because Macaskie was denied any form of book to read. He remembered afterwards: 'At home I had been reading for the Bar, and all this seemed so much time wasted.'[11]

The cobbler who helped them was named Leonidas Karagiannopoulos and he was the secretary of the EAM (National Liberation Front) in Vathi. He made the shoes for Macaskie and hid in their soles twenty gold pounds that Rees had sent for this purpose, before they were smuggled in by the courageous Synanidou. Macaskie would never forget the help that he received from Irenios, and later in the war would send him a letter full of gratitude and warm thanks. The group remained on Samos for eight months in total, as their trial was repeatedly postponed, and it was probably during this period that Macaskie (who had leaned a little Ancient Greek at school) became fluent in the modern language following tuition from Alexis. Eventually, in March 1943 they were ordered to Athens. Immediately after Easter 1943, an Italian submarine transported the prisoners to Leros and from there to Rhodes, from whence they were taken by ship to Piraeus. In the cells of Kallithea prison, established by the Nazis in 1941 in a converted school to hold resistance fighters, they were locked up. Here they met Commander Emmanuele Vernicos, a fellow MI9 and 'A' Force operative, who was also awaiting trial. A remarkable photograph was smuggled out of the prison showing Macaskie and Vernicos together. There, now, they awaited their fate. At the same time, concern was growing ever stronger for Macaskie's welfare at 'A' Force headquarters, because news had just been received in Cairo of the execution by the Italians of another captured British agent, Lieutenant John Atkinson.

The interests of the British in Greece at this time were being represented by the Swiss Legation, and on 22 March the Swiss Consul Charles-Edouard de Bavier visited Macaskie to ascertain his state of health. In his report to the Swiss Foreign Ministry he noted: 'Captain Macaskie does not complain about his treatment but gave me a list of items that he needs (tooth brush, soap) and asks for books. These things I will deliver to him tomorrow.'[12]

On 7 April 1943, proceedings began to try Macaskie as a spy, and for using unauthorised radio equipment, and subsequent to this de Bavier approached a number of high-ranking Italians to argue his case. One of these was Colonel Antonio Pignatelli, aide de camp to the Supreme Italian commander in Greece, General Carlo Geloso. Although he was sympathetic to a number of the arguments de Bavier put forward, he was doubtful that Macaskie would be granted prisoner of war status, for the simple fact that when captured he was wearing a pullover over his military shirt, and his trousers were not recognisably those of a British officer. De Bavier had argued that his lightweight shirt was standard issue for officers in the Egyptian theatre, and he had worn a pullover because it was cold on board the boat in which he was attempting to escape. Ironically, Macaskie also at this stage told him that he was not seeking prisoner of war status, as that would probably result in him being transferred to Italy. The conditions in which he was living at that time were also possibly better than he might expect as a PoW. De Bavier also wrote to Macaskie's mother, under date 9 April 1943:

> I have succeeded in my capacity as representative of your country in visiting your son three times since he was brought to Athens to the Callitea [Kallithea] prison. I brought him the objects that I thought would bring him the most pleasure and he asked me today to inform you of the state of his health. He is well and is undergoing his rather severe detention very courageously since unfortunately he is not considered a prisoner of war, not having been captured in uniform. I have however taken steps to obtain for him the treatment he would be entitled to receive as an English officer, based on the fact that when he was captured he was wearing under his pullover a shirt with the insignia of his rank. I will not fail to return to see your son as often as I can and to continue to bring him books and vitamins, 'Jemalt',

> 'Redoxon' etc. Being a father myself, I think of your concerns as a mother with special sympathy, but I want to believe that after this long painful time of trials you will finally be able, thanks to divine protection, to find yourselves reunited.[13]

Shortly afterwards, an attempt was made by the British to begin a dialogue with the Italian government through the Vatican office in Beirut, the Vatican being in effect a neutral state. That same month, British intelligence in Istanbul also tried a similar appeal. The initiative for securing the release of the young British officer appears to have been taken by General Henry Maitland Wilson, commander of British forces in the Middle East. One of his staff officers, Colonel Thompson approached Archbishop Angelo Giuseppe Roncalli the papal nuncio in Istanbul, to take on the case. In a cipher telegram categorised as 'Most Secret' Thompson reported:

> Must warn you that in order to show Vatican that approach was genuine Archbishop insisted on starting his signal in following terms: "The British Government through the intermediary of Col Thompson acting on behalf of General Wilson C in C Middle East asks intervention etc." If this should come to ears of Embassy here which is possible but not likely Ambassador will not be pleased as he has no knowledge of approach … if there is any comeback I shall take line that approach was a purely private one and that I had no idea of what impression Archbishop may or may not have given Vatican regarding

> status ... Archbishop considers it certain that if Macaskie has not confessed to espionage or sabotage and he is under Italian control the approach will be successful. If however he has confessed or is under German control, especially latter, Archbishop is very dubious.[14]

A curious aspect of this matter was the fact that the Italians appeared to believe that Macaskie was Wilson's nephew. Whether this was a deliberate deception by the British, or simply a misunderstanding, is not clear. The British government made no protest against the accusation for which Macaskie was on trial, because he was in civilian clothes at the time of his arrest. Instead, their approach was simply a humanitarian one and an attempt to save his life. If the Italian government would consider the approach, then the British would offer to release five Italian soldiers who had been captured under circumstances which would also render them liable to charges of espionage or sabotage. The men in question were Francesco Furetta, Enrico Milani and Alessandro Mantovani, who had parachuted into Syria with radio equipment on 21 December 1942, as well as Pasquale Ricciardo and Policarpo Tito who had landed by parachute on Cyprus, similarly equipped. The British asked that the Holy See would, if necessary, also take matters up with the German authorities. The matter was passed to Vatican Secretary of State Luigi Maglione, who in turn contacted the Italian Ambassador to the Vatican. A report and update on the request was passed to Hugh Montgomery, Secretary of the British Legation to the Holy See on 6 May 1943.

Macaskie would have a loyal ally in Montgomery. During the war he repeatedly exploited the neutral status of the Vatican, by helping numerous Allied servicemen to escape from fascist-controlled territory. Despite the criticism of many senior churchmen, he continued these activities and gained the nickname 'the battling diplomat' as a result. A few days later a further request was made by the British that the Holy Father should also intercede to try to obtain better treatment for Macaskie, who it was understood was being held in solitary confinement with poor clothing and inadequate food, which it was feared would damage his heath. The matter was passed to the ambassador of the Kingdom of Italy to the Vatican who confirmed that the matter had received attention at the highest level, and although due to the circumstances of his capture, Macaskie was not granted the status of prisoner of war, should a capital sentence be passed against him it was assured that this would be suspended.

By now, Macaskie's case had reached the highest levels of the British government. On 5 June Hugh Montgomery wrote to Maglione to inform him that no lesser figure than Foreign Secretary Anthony Eden had requested that the British Minister of State at Cairo begin detailed plans for the hand-over for the five Italians who were being offered in exchange. This it was envisaged would take place in Turkey, with the parties being delivered to their respective embassies simultaneously.

However on 15 June the Italian government now claimed that there had been a misunderstanding – perhaps not surprising considering the tortuous diplomatic channels involved. It claimed that the British government had at first offered the five captured Italians in exchange for Macaskie's life. Now, the British wanted Macaskie released in exchange for the five Italians. This they said was not acceptable, as it would place Macaskie who was captured in civilian clothes and charged with 'terrorist' acts on an equal footing with the five paratroopers, who were captured in uniform in an open and obvious military action. The note concluded that the Italian government had deferred the death sentence out of respect for the wishes of the Holy See, but if the British government persisted with its requests, then it would be forced to reconsider! Pressure was also being put on the Italians from another direction, however. In Turkey, Noël Rees, head of N Section operations here, also contacted Roncalli, and let it be known that if Macaskie was executed, twenty Italian prisoners of war would be shot in retaliation. This however seems to have been a bluff on his part; it is doubtful he had access to twenty Italian prisoners and certainly lacked the authority to have them shot.

Perhaps the greatest of Macaskie's stays at this time were the letters that he regularly received from his sister Nadine. One of Frank's replies, dated 10 June 1943, survives. Sent from the Kallithea prison, it reads:

> I am getting two or three letters a week now, so am feeling very happy indeed. Within the last week I have had a letter from Audrey, Mary Parker, George and the Chief Clerk at the County Office, and the most pleasing

> thing is that they are taking little more than a month to get here. Indeed the one from Thompson, the Chief Clerk took less than a month. I am rather worried though about the length of time it is taking my letters to get to England. I wrote to many people as soon as I got here at the beginning of March & yet none of you writing at the end of April and Thompson on 12 May have mentioned having received letters from me, and I have also learned that a letter which I wrote to the Red Cross here in Athens has taken near three months to arrive – it has only had to travel three miles! So I am wondering and worrying how long my letters will take to reach England. I have asked the Red Cross to enquire into the delay & I am hoping that this & future letters will travel much faster. Please tell Mother this & also that in future I shall be writing on Fridays instead of Sundays with the same object in view. By the way I have just realised that the number I have been putting on my letters – 121772 – is probably not a PoW number at all, or if it is it is my old German one. Is it maybe my own British service number which I could never remember! So it will be better not to use it. I am sorry fags are so expensive, you mustn't dream of sending me any – I get all I need.[15]

From information in the Swiss diplomatic archives it is also clear that the Swiss embassy in London was acting as a conduit for correspondence, and had also forwarded a letter from Nadine as well as one from Reverend H.A. Wareham, Vicar of Horsforth.

After several delays, it was suddenly announced on 5 July 1943 that five days later Macaskie was to be put on trial by the Italian occupying forces, in particular a Military War Tribunal of the 11th Italian Army. He was accused of being:

> [An] enemy agent in that he tried, in agreement with English spy organisations and with the collaboration of Greek accomplices to round up English troops escaped from concentration camps or running away from imprisonment, in the period of the invasion of Greece by Axis troops: he was successful in the cases of two escaped English soldiers, Natusch Roy Spencer and Trevor Joannes [sic] Francis Stevens.[16]

He was further charged:

> For the offence committed against article 385 of the Penal Code in that at about 10.00pm on the 6/7/1942, whilst in the prison of Vathi (Samos) under preventative detention for an offence subject to the jurisdiction of the Italian Military Authority, he escaped and was recaptured at about 12.30am on the 7th day of the same month in the courtyard of the nearby general headquarters.[17]

Ladas meanwhile was arraigned thus:

> For having given aid and information to the English army captain Francis Gilbert Macaskie, enemy agent, acting as his interpreter in Greek territory occupied by

> Italian forces from 20/11/1941, date of the departure from Chesmet [Çeşme] (Asia Minor) until 4/1/1942, date on which he was arrested by Italian troops.[18]

Swiss Consul de Bavier immediately tried to intervene on Macaskie's behalf. He arranged to see the senior Italian officer in Athens, General Carlo Vecchiarelli (who had succeeded Geloso in May) to appraise him of some important facts. These were firstly that the Italians had already executed one British officer the previous year, and this had caused extreme dismay in British government circles, secondly that there were as many as 300,000 Italian prisoners currently in British hands who might suffer reprisals, and thirdly that there were Italian officers currently operating in civilian clothes in Ethiopia. If Macaskie was shot, these men could expect the same treatment. Lastly, he pointed out that a German officer named Hadamschek had been captured by the British in North Africa, not in civilian clothes, but actually in one of their uniforms. He had been convicted of spying, and sentenced to death. However the sentence was commuted and he was instead sent to a prisoner of war camp in Canada. De Bavier told Vecchiarelli that he recommended the Italians treat Macaskie with clemency, not out of any sense of sentimentality but in their own self-interest.

The following day he spoke with Pellegrino Ghigi, Italian Plenipotentiary in Athens, and argued that on account of his young age, Ladas should not be tried at all. He also suggested that the trial should be postponed, because the presiding officer the Italian general Gherardo Magaldi was known to be particularly severe, but he was also rumoured to be due to leave Athens soon. He was told that Magaldi would not be leaving, and that he was indeed severe but also just. In any case, once the trial process had started it must continue. De Bavier asked that Macaskie be provided with a good lawyer, as was his right under Article 62 of the Geneva Convention. In his report to the Swiss government, he continued:

> 8 July – I go to Callitea [Kallithea] Prison with Major Corti to see Macaskie, who is always very calm and brave. He doesn't think about himself, but about the other men captured with him. Major Corti and I make him write the usual request for a lawyer and Major Corti strongly recommends that he take Lieutenant Chiaraviglio whom he knows and who he says is very capable. I will go myself in the afternoon to fetch this lawyer from his home and take him to Callitea prison … I do not need to receive a copy of the notification document because I have already read it in prison with Macaskie. I was able to see that he is being prosecuted for escaping and for having sought, on his return to Greece to enable his comrades who had also escaped from prison to flee to Egypt. He therefore did not seek to organise resistance bands and he never used firearms like Atkinson who was shot in February. His lawyer however informs me that the Italian Military Penal code already provides the death penalty for an enemy officer simply for being arrested in time of war in civilian clothes in the Kingdom of Italy or its occupied territories.[19]

When he returned to the prison, Macaskie thanked de Bavier in the most touching terms for everything that he had done for him. The trial of the three accused was indeed conducted by the presiding officer of the Italian Military Court, General Gherardo Magaldi, who was sometimes called 'Vabene', because he often used the expression '*va bene*' (meaning 'it's OK'). Magaldi was lame, crippled by a wound in the First World War, and had two sons killed in the Second, one in Albania and one on the Russian front. De Bavier reported:

> From the opening of the debates in the Military Tribunal it was foreseeable that things would go badly, in that General Magaldi would not admit any of the arguments of the interested parties, and did not take any account of their answers, except to criticise the words of Macaskie and his advocate on the subject of the wearing of uniform, which were considered by the President of the Tribunal to be of no importance. For him, the only fact that counted was that Captain Macaskie wore a pullover over his military shirt which hid it. Macaskie's lawyer spoke well, insisting on the fact that the wearing of an English officer's military shirt, which included on the shoulders epaulets showing his pips of rank, must be considered as sufficient argument for Macaskie to be treated as a prisoner of war, with all the consequences that would result for his fate. At the end of his plea he asked for a measure of clemency in favour of Macaskie, recalling that this measure would have a favourable repercussion

> on the Italians who were taken prisoner in similar circumstances as him in Ethiopia. General Magaldi did not seem to listen to Captain Chiaraviglio's plea.[20]

During the trial, Macaskie's courage was an inspiration to his co-accused. In particular, Francis Jones states that Chrysinis as a young man had been a callow youth, frequently frightened and in his words 'no hero'. Yet he also avers that in the weeks and months under the threat of a death sentence, he grew within him a core of steel, undoubtedly drawing strength from the example set by Macaskie. Fellow prisoner Alexis Ladas confirms this assertion in his own account of the court proceedings. Ladas states:

> Our trial, involving an English captain as it did, was quite an occasion in occupied Athens. For propaganda reasons it was thrown open to the public and was attended by everybody who was anybody. Captain Macaskie my English cellmate, behaved splendidly. He was completely fearless and even taunted the judges though he knew it might cost him his life. In less than half an hour the judges had returned. All four colonels as well as the presiding general, whose chins had previously been grey with stubble, were freshly shaven. Clearly, arriving at a verdict had not demanded too much soul searching of them. The president put on his hat and stood up to pronounce sentence on Captain Macaskie. 'Condannato a la pena di morte median fucilazione al petto,' he intoned. Frank was to die with his chest full of holes.

> Frank smiled his imperturbable, almost deprecating smile. Then my turn came and I drew myself up stiff to attention. I think I could have died quite well at that moment. 'Condannato a la pena di morte median fucilazione a la schiena.' Having been captured in civilian clothes I was to be shot in the back in the dishonourable manner reserved for spies. I was utterly and completely shattered.[21]

Natalia Mela, a relation of Ladas, was a witness to the trial. When the death sentence was passed, she remembered through streaming tears seeing Macaskie, a hand in pocket, looking superbly nonchalant, his expression betraying satisfied superiority whilst in her eyes Alexis was as defiant as a lion. On 10 July, the decision was published: Macaskie, Ladas and Chrysinis were all sentenced to death by firing squad three days hence. The first, as a military officer, was to face the firing squad. Both Chrysinis, and Ladas, regarded as civilians, were to be shot in the back. The four convicts were transferred from Kallithea prison to the infamous Averoff gaol, where three were locked up in death row cells, in the basement, while Trypanis, who received a lighter punishment, was on the upper floor. Journalist Richard Capell was told that later,

> … in the Callitea Prison, when Macaskie was brought back from his trial, other inmates included Achilleas Kyrou of the newspaper *Estia*. They had a party, someone managing to produce a bottle of wine; and Kyrou remembers Macaskie singing foxtrots. The next day,

> when the condemned men were taken off to the Averoff prison, all the Callitea captives joined in shouting: Zito O Frank – Hail Frank![22]

Shortly after the trial, Magaldi would be recalled from the Military Court in Athens to Italy, due to his excessive severity in sentencing. After Italy's collapse he would join Mussolini in the Italian Social Republic, the Nazi puppet state in the north, and in 1946 would be arraigned as a war criminal for his actions in Dalmatia. After the verdict the Swiss redoubled their efforts on behalf of Macaskie, and these were all the more effective because pressure was simultaneously being applied by their Legation in Rome on behalf of the British government. The Swiss Consul there was able to report on 27 July that:

> I have been in daily contact with General Gandini, Chief of Staff of General Vecchiarelli, who has shown the greatest understanding in this painful affair and who has certainly influenced his superior in a benevolent direction. It could also be that General Vecchiarelli received instructions from the Chigi Palace to spare the life of Captain Macaskie, but did not want to tell me about it, wanting to make me feel that the favour he was granting me was personal and very valuable … It was only on Thursday 16th July at 7.00pm, after six days of anxious waiting, that General Gandini finally announced to me that his chief had accepted the requests for a pardon of this English officer and the two Greeks who were captured with him, the young lad Ladas and the

> captain of the ship on which they escaped. I had in fact also insisted on the pardon of the other two interested parties, because Macaskie very nobly declared that he would refuse any favour not granted to his two friends.[23]

By late July the British government, via the British Legation at the Vatican was pressing for a date for the prisoner exchange, no further word having been heard from the Italians since late in the previous month. On 3 August 1943, under the heading Most Immediate, D.G. Osborne of the British Legation wrote to Cardinal Maglione:

> I now have the honour, under instructions from His Majesty's Principal Secretary of State for Foreign Affairs [Anthony Eden] to make the following urgent appeal to Your Eminence on behalf of this officer.
>
> Recent developments in the case of Captain Macaskie were, I am now informed by the Foreign Office, as follows. Some weeks ago the Swiss Chargé d'Affaires at Athens was suddenly informed that Captain Macaskie would be tried on July 10th. He failed to secure the officer's recognition as a prisoner of war and, after a trial of four and a half hours, which the Chargé d'Affaires attended, Macaskie and the two Greeks caught with him were sentenced to death.

After the trial the Chargé d'Affaires called on the Italian Commanding General by whose Chief of Staff he was assured in strict confidence that, despite the death sentence passed on Macaskie his position was not hopeless and his appeal would be considered immediately. The Swiss Government believe that it has not yet been examined.

In these circumstances the Swiss Government have been asked, through their legation in Rome, to support the appeal made by Captain Macaskie against his death sentence by all the means in their power. As the Swiss Government have been informed, His Majesty's Government are ready to deliver in Turkey the five Italians, to whose exchange the Italian Government were believed to have agreed, as a result of the intervention of the Holy See, on any date the Italian Government may choose, provided that they will deliver Captain Macaskie on the same date.

… as a result of His Holiness' intervention the Italian authorities undertook that, if sentence of death were passed on the above-mentioned officer, it should not be carried out.… it was moreover stated that the [Italian] authorities had agreed to commute the sentence which should be passed on this officer. I therefore have the honour to beg that Your Eminence will, in the name of His Holiness, be so good as to intervene immediately and energetically with a view to ensuring that Captain

> Macaskie's sentence is commuted, pardon granted to him, and the arrangement accepted whereby he may be exchanged for the five Italians mentioned.[24]

The Vatican duly passed on the request, two days later, but here the involvement of the Holy See in the Macaskie case appears to end. Dramatic events were now taking place elsewhere in Italy. In July the Allies had invaded Sicily, and later that month the first Allied bombs fell on Rome. Mussolini had been deposed on 25 July, and Italy would soon be out of the war as an Axis combatant nation. As far as Macaskie and his comrades in the condemned cells of the Averoff prison were concerned, they were only at first aware of the fact that the executions originally fixed for 13 July 1943 were repeatedly postponed. On 15 August Frank again wrote to his sister Nadine, a letter which conveyed little or no sense of alarm about the position he was in:

> Your talk of cricket gives me many happy memories. I can think of nothing which would make me forget the war & prisons & trials & so on so effectively as a game of cricket. There is something so peaceful and clean and so English about it. You ask about the weather here. I think I am right in saying that Greece and Southern Italy are the most pleasant climates in the world. Here in Greece from April till November you get unbroken sunshine without it being too hot. You can arrange a picnic two or three months ahead and be quite certain that you will have a perfect day. I am talking about the

> weather out of doors of course. Here in this blasted [?] cell the heat is dreadful at times because there is only a tiny barred window far above my head and with the door perpetually locked there is very little ventilation. However I am allowed out for exercise each morning and evening, and the exercise yard is the nicest I have come across so far – and by now I have quite a wide experience of prisons: this is the tenth I have been in! In this yard there two lovely trees, a big mulberry & a Eucalyptus, and it is very pleasant to sit underneath them and read. Oddly enough there are quite a lot of advantages of being under sentence of death! Many Athenian friends have been most kind to me. They turned up in force at my trial, and since I have been in the condemned cell I have received a bottle of whisky and a bottle of gin as well as many less wonderful presents! You can imagine what pleasures I have had. If I get out of this mess Nadine, as I am sure I shall, then luck will have been amazing and with such luck I know it can't be long before I see you all again.[25]

The impact of the prolonged spell in prison perhaps had a permanent effect on Macaskie. Certainly his friend Georgios Seferiades believed so, and wrote later:

> On those very rare occasions that he talked about that period, his voice had a bruised tone, a tone of wounded freedom, if I may so put it. It was prison that cut short for a time that vigorous élan which drew him out of

> himself towards the thing that he considered right: it was the four walls that force us to look within ourselves at the inexhaustible despair of human conditions.[26]

It was not until 9 September that the prisoners learned of Italy's imminent collapse, but this was not unalloyed good news. The Italian authorities in Athens were clearly vacillating over the executions, but if the Germans took over, they were a very different proposition, and were likely to empty the condemned cells of Averoff in their usual thorough fashion. It became imperative – once again – that Frank and the others should escape. The Italian guards were now hesitant, unsure which side to back. Macaskie took advantage of this, offering to take with him all those who wished to change sides. To those who wanted to desert, he promised help to reach the Middle East (a promise he kept). The flight of these Italian officers from Lavrio, a village outside Athens, was undertaken by the 'Aliki' organisation and personally overseen by Konstantinos Doxiadis. Disguised as a peasant, like the Italians, he carried them in a cart to the place where they boarded a boat.

The gold sovereigns in the boots given to him on Samos by the Bishop also came into their own at this point, in persuading the guards to unlock the cells. Macaskie, Chrysinis and Alexis walked out of the prison without a shot being fired, a car driven by Xavier de Bavier (son of the Swiss consul) was waiting for them outside Averoff and took them to the Swiss Legation. Only Trypanis did not manage to escape, because he was unlucky and ran into a Fascist guard. After a few days he tried again, but this time he was shot in the leg and was transferred to the Municipal Hospital, on Akadimias Street. Finally, he was released after Thomashausen's appeal to Rino Rossi, who had by then been transferred from Rhodes to Athens.

However, they were by no means out of danger; the Germans began looking for Macaskie as soon as they realised that he had escaped. It was too risky to remain together, so the group split up. Frank stayed at the Swiss consul's house in Athens, and he remembered later that he enjoyed a memorable, delicious dinner that evening, served with champagne, which must have made for quite a contrast with the prison fare upon which he had survived up to that point. As far as the Swiss ambassador was concerned, he firmly believed that he was correct in arranging to collect Macaskie, in that he was acting under Article 75 of the Geneva Convention which states that when an Armistice is concluded, prisoners must be immediately released. However he was also aware that his actions in sheltering Macaskie could be seen as stretching the boundaries of his country's famed neutrality, and he later wrote to his Foreign Minister:

> I was well aware of the danger of receiving this officer, but in certain circumstances of life you will certainly recognise, as I do, that honour must take precedence over all other considerations. Since the protection of British interests has been entrusted to us, it would have been treason on my part to have thrown Macaskie into the street, that is to have delivered him up to the principal enemies of his country. I truly believe that none of my colleagues has found themselves in such a compromising situation, which unfortunately could happen again at any

> moment, other Englishmen having managed to escape from Italian prisons before they were occupied by troops of the Reich. I add that I would have acted the same way towards a German officer, had the roles been reversed. I am therefore pleased to believe that you will approve of my actions.[27]

However Macaskie had been with him only twenty-four hours when, later that night an unknown voice on the telephone warned him to get out. The Gestapo, Germany's feared secret police, were on their way. He left just in time, and was given shelter by Archbishop Damaskinos of Athens. Macaskie had contacted his legal adviser Giannis Georgakis, who introduced him to the Archbishop. Initially the Germans thought he might be at the Archbishop's office in Athens, and ransacked the place, leaving upturned drawers and papers all over the floor. After being offered sanctuary under his roof, the fugitive British officer stayed for two weeks, with German officers paying formal calls at the house during that time. One hair raising incident, demonstrating Damaskinos' calmness under pressure, is described by Ioanna Tsatsou, the Archbishop's assistant:

> This afternoon, whilst he was calmly chatting at his home, 'Germans', rang out the voice of his servant as he opened the door of his office. He barely managed to pass the Englishman into the next room. Four senior German officers were there. He was able to receive them coolly and politely. They came to officially apologise for the morning investigation and left immediately. When

> from the wide window he saw their car disappearing down the avenue he sat down in an armchair with deep relief. Macaskie also entered and they continued their conversation about the political groups. In the evening we went up to Psychiko to see Themistocles Tsatsos [Ioanna's brother in law who was offering temporary shelter] and met Macaskie. Cultivated, polite, and reminiscent of Lord Byron, he loves Greece like his own country.[28]

In late September 1943, the Greek government, through Archbishop Damaskinos, asked Aggelos Evert the chief of the Athens police to help Macaskie flee Greece. Evert duly assisted in smuggling him out to Cairo. The occupation authorities had long suspected Evert's loyalties, and for this reason had relieved him of his duties in July 1943. However, they were forced to reinstate him in a very short space of time, after the reaction to this that occurred within the police force. Now Evert, in full dress uniform, escorted Macaskie in his official police car with its pennants flying to Lavrio, managing to get him through the German roadblocks and thereby save him again. Macaskie said later: 'I don't know how he kept his nerve under the Germans, helping us the whole time.'[29]

It was not plain sailing all the way however. The plan was to take Macaskie to meet an agent who would be travelling by bus, and who would then take him on the final part of the journey to a hidden inlet, where he would embark for Smyrna once more. The rendezvous was to be a bus station, where the signal the agent would give would be to hold a chicken out of the window (this was not in fact as bizarre as it sounds – Greek villagers often travelled by bus with their hens). Bus after bus passed by, but no chicken appeared. To avert suspicion as to why they were lingering, Evert told his driver to get under the bonnet and start tinkering with the engine, which he did. As time went on however, Evert and Georgakis who was with him, decided they had better return to Athens before inquisitive passers-by started offering to help start the car. As Macaskie got out, his 'black moustache' was beginning to run down his chin, but luckily his contact soon arrived.

Evert was, on the face of it, an ambiguous character. Of German descent, he spent most of the war hunting communists and co-operating with the occupying forces, whilst at the same time staying in contact with the Greek government in exile, and helping Jews to escape, for which he was later to be regarded as Righteous Among the Nations. He stated that he drew his inspiration from the words and deeds of Archbishop Damaskinos. Some twenty-six British evaders were said to owe their freedom to Evert, and whilst Macaskie was at large in Athens after his first escape, he tried to protect him by means of a discreet bodyguard.

Damaskinos for his part had come to be Archbishop via a roundabout route. Now aged 52, he had been first elected to the See in 1938, but Metaxas, dictator of Greece had opposed his ordination, installing instead Bishop Chrysanthos in his place. After the German invasion of 1941, Chrysanthos was himself ejected after he failed to support the quisling Greek government, and with Axis approval Damaskinos was re-instated. However, he proved himself to be no friend of the occupiers, and frequently clashed with them. He sent his lawyer Georgakis (who had trained in Germany) to argue for Greek prisoners in German military courts, and he protested strongly and publicly against the deportation of the Greek Jews to Auschwitz, to a degree unique among churchmen in occupied countries and earning him also the title Righteous Among the Nations after the war. When the local SS commander threatened to put him before a firing squad, he reminded him that in the Greek tradition prelates were hanged rather than shot, and asked him to respect local customs. He was an ex-soldier himself, having enlisted in the Greek army during the Balkan wars of the early twentieth century.

Damaskinos however had recently grown alarmed at the increasing strength of the communist element of the resistance movement in his country. The Greek resistance to German occupation was split into a kaleidoscope of different factions, reflecting all shades of political opinion from monarchist to republican to communist. Early on the British had found the communist group ELAS to be among the strongest, and had channelled weapons to them. They had also acquired weapons from the enemy, having disarmed an entire Italian division when Italy collapsed. Almost as powerful were Colonel Napoleon Zervas' EDES, a republican group also supported by the British, parts of which had Nazi sympathies. The Germans had meanwhile created right-wing Security Battalions from among the Greeks, and had them trained by the SS, to hunt communists. Whilst Greek was killing Greek, they reasoned, they were not killing Germans. Increasingly the resistance groups were fighting amongst themselves.

Furthermore, there were reports that ELAS were now hoarding guns and personnel in preparation for an attempted takeover, and Damaskinos feared that this might well happen in the power vacuum left in the wake of the now inevitable German withdrawal in the coming year.

His other main concern was that if King George II attempted to return to Greece (which he had fled in the face of the Axis invasion) without a popular mandate, this could only enflame the situation. Some historians view Frank Macaskie's stay with the archbishop over a ten-day period in September 1943, and the numerous discussions that they had regarding the creation of anti-Communist coalition, as the beginning of the hierarch's candidacy for regent. Certainly the conversations between Macaskie, Damaskinos, and the archbishop's close friend, chief of police Aggelos Evert, gave the former confidence in his ability to serve as the leading figure in Greece after the German withdrawal, which testifies both to the strength of his personality and the influence that the church still retained among all political elements in Greece. Evert meanwhile had assured Macaskie that the Athens police force was large and reliable, but unarmed. If it was to be armed by the British, then it could both maintain order and ensure that any plebiscite regarding the future of the monarchy was carried out fairly. When Macaskie arrived back in Cairo, he carried a report which he had prepared on Damaskinos for Middle East Headquarters:

> There is only one man in Greece – by reason of his very high personal prestige which has been greatly enhanced

> by his magnificent work and example during the period of enemy occupation, and also because he, as head of the Church in Greece, is more or less above politics and admired by all political parties – who can induce these various political groups and patriotic organisations to work together against the Germans, and after the liberation prevent grave internal dissension … This man is the Archbishop of Athens and Primate of Greece Damaskinos.[30]

Damaskinos' personality and courageous work during the first two years of the occupation were duly noted in the report. Equally important was his ability to avoid becoming involved in the growing struggle between the various resistance movements throughout Greece. While Macaskie may have overestimated the archbishop's 'apolitical' stance, his ability to conceal his fears of the left in public, in spite of the consistent pressure to denounce the communist-led EAM-ELAS, led all sides to accept him as the only individual who possessed both the prestige and influence to prevent civil war. Macaskie, of course, excluded the communists from 'the political groups and patriotic organisations' referenced in his statement. In common with much of British intelligence he too was beginning to see ELAS as a threat. In addition to his report about his conversations with Damaskinos and his allies, Macaskie passed on a memorandum from the archbishop regarding the situation in Greece and plans for the immediate post-occupation period. Damaskinos' message to British officials betrayed both his concerns about the communists, and his own growing power in Athens. His first request was that he should establish contact with British government representatives in Cairo to ensure the prevention of internal disintegration following a German withdrawal from the country, which appeared to many a foregone conclusion: 'Now that the liberation of Greece appears to be imminent he would like to have close liaison with GHQ Middle East and authority from the British Government to act in certain ways which he is confident will ensure the unity of the Greek people at a time when internal dissension would be disastrous.'[31]

Clearly Damaskinos in a little more than two short years had emerged as a powerful personality, and the hope of many old school politicians of the traditional parties, who feared the potential power and designs of the communists in the postwar period in Greece. His position regarding the communist threat was also left in no doubt in this report. Regarding the communists, he warned, 'that the strength of the Communist Party in Greece not be underrated. It is, in fact, numerous, widespread though chiefly in Athens, Piraeus and Salonika and well organised.'[32]

Damaskinos viewed the current power of the communists as ephemeral and chiefly a consequence of the effect of war upon Greece. However he also realised that a German withdrawal would create an opportunity for them and leave the capital vulnerable to a communist takeover.

> But he believes that it is chiefly a product of the enemy occupation and hunger … and that with the presence … of Allied troops and enough food the number of

> communists will slowly but steadily diminish. But at the moment this danger is great … If, as seems possible and even probable, the Germans withdraw to the North of Greece before there is an Allied landing, there is nothing whatever to prevent the communists from taking control of Athens and Piraeus.[33]

Because there were no other forces capable of challenging such a move, he hoped the Allies could send weapons and supplies to arm a local force under Athens police chief Aggelos Evert. In addition to this, he suggested that upon a German withdrawal the British should draft a statement regarding the position of the archbishop. In this eventuality,

> the Commander in Chief Middle East should announce … the Archbishop of Greece, Damaskinos, with the Chief of Police will be responsible for the order and Government … until the arrival of the Greek Government or an Allied Military Governor … Evert suggested that weapons should be sent in to arm the Athens police forces. Col. Evert has at his disposal a force of 3,000 and he can guarantee the support of these men in the event of trouble.[34]

Macaskie, Damaskinos, and others hoped that, 'with this authority, the combination of the Head of the Greek Church, the chief of police, and a British officer, backed by an armed police force, will probably be sufficient to prevent even the beginning of trouble'.[35]

This optimistic report of circumstances on the ground and the viability of this plan were however shortsighted. Denis S. Laskey, a British Foreign Office official working in the Southern Department recognised that this policy could ignite civil war in the immediate postwar period. For this reason, he dismissed the plan of creating an anti-communist resistance bloc in preparation for the liberation of Greece. However, Damaskinos remained the strongest option for maintaining some sort of stability in that country. Indeed, by 1943 Damaskinos had become more of a politician than he was a cleric, although the two roles were seldom mutually exclusive in modern Greek politics. Still, the circumstances of the occupation and his own personality surpassed even the accepted norms of the 'political hierarch'. The archbishop's requests regarding the establishment of a regency were based on the firmly established belief among most Athenian politicians that the King would not be welcomed in Greece, until the issue of his fate could be decided in some form of referendum.

> During the interim between the liberation of Greece and the end of the war or such time as the promised plebiscite ... can be held, His eminence will do all in his power to preserve unity in Greece and prevent political dissensions ... He urges ... that the King should not return to Greece until after such plebiscite; that he should remain King of Greece, work for Greece and represent Greece at Allied Conferences, but not return to the country.[36]

In the event, civil war had begun in Greece anyway by late 1943, and clashes between ELAS and EDES that year forced the British government to reconsider the possibility of a regency; British Foreign Secretary Anthony Eden raised the topic with King George II. The latter agreed to reconsider the timing of his return to Greece, but refused initially to consider any suspension of his reign. He articulated his new stance in a letter to Emmanouil Tsouderos, Prime Minister and head of the Greek government in exile, on 8 November 1943. However the language he used regarding his return appeared vague enough to allow politicians in Athens to view the letter as evidence of the King's acceptance of a plebiscite to resolve the constitutional crisis. This prompted the politicians to send a letter to Tsouderos approving the letter from the King in January 1944. In response, the Greek Prime Minister sent a letter to Damaskinos requesting that he make an appeal for reconciliation and to open negotiations with Athenian politicians on behalf of the Cairo government, which, Tsouderos emphasised, was and should remain the only legitimate Greek administration. In the meantime, Colonel Christopher Woodhouse, a British officer serving in the Allied Military Mission in Greece, negotiated with the three major resistance bands, ELAS, EDES, and EKKA a temporary halt to the civil war, better known as the Plaka Agreement, on 29 February 1944.

Chapter Five

With MI9 Again

In early 1944, military developments on the Eastern Front began to concern those in the British government who were involved in Greek affairs. It was now evident that the Red Army would soon be moving westwards and southward into the Balkans. Once the Soviets entered Bulgaria, they might continue into Greece, either in pursuit of the Germans, or if the Germans had already left, as a result of their own momentum. Churchill in particular was aware of the danger of communist 'infusion' of the Balkans. This would lead eventually to his 'spheres of influence' approach to Stalin, when in October he would travel without Roosevelt to Moscow, to try to preserve British hegemony in the Mediterranean in the postwar world. On a scrap of paper, Churchill offered to allow the Soviet dictator a free hand in eastern Europe, in particular Rumania, in exchange for recognition of Greece as within Britain's purview. As Churchill was later to put it, Greece was the brand that he pulled from the burning. In the event, Stalin would honour the agreement, and in 1944 and 1945 at least would not offer support to the communist EAM/ELAS faction in Greece. However at this point, the threat posed by them seemed to the British to be extremely serious, and this would greatly influence the course of events on the ground for MI9.

Late September 1943 had found Macaskie in Ankara. Here he wrote a heartfelt letter of thanks to Commander Wolfson, for his efforts not just in getting him away from Athens earlier in the month, but throughout the time that he had been a prisoner in Italian hands. In it he stated:

> I am, and always shall be, very deeply grateful to you. This feeling of gratitude is not prompted by the final satisfactory result of your efforts: it has been with me the whole time and would have been the same whatever may have been the result. I have known all the time that you were doing everything possible to help me; and this knowledge has meant a very great deal to me.[1]

He and Ladas also jointly presented an engraved silver snuff box to Noël Rees, as a sign of their gratitude for all that he had done behind the scenes. When Frank arrived in Cairo, a joyous family re-union awaited him. His brother John was there, on leave from his duties as a radio operator in the Merchant Navy, as was his sister Audrey who was in the WRNS. Around about this time, he was recommended for a bar to his Military Cross which would eventually be announced six months later, on 23 March 1944, in the *London Gazette*. For reasons of secrecy, no citation was ever published for this award, which is simply stated as being for Special Operations, Middle East. In December he was granted leave in the UK, to the delight of his widowed mother. It was not purely for compassionate reasons that he was sent home, however. His MI9 file makes it clear that Macaskie returned to Cairo greatly enthused by his time with Damaskinos and his efforts to create a unified anti-communist resistance front in his country, and his approach to the British Embassy to Greece about this raised some eyebrows, as the British government was yet to be convinced of the merits of a Damaskinos regency. His 'handler' Tony Simonds wrote that Dudley Clarke's deputy Noël Wild:

> … very wisely sent [Macaskie] home to England on leave, not only to recover his physical health, but also to regain his mental stability. That is to say political mental stability as it was felt that coming directly from Greece, and having been so long connected with Greek affairs he should be given a fair opportunity to see the forest for the trees and also get up to date with other things going on in the world. In fairness to Macaskie I think he has most certainly done this and now has an extremely sensible and practical outlook on Greece.[2]

During his time in the UK Macaskie also met Brigadier Norman Crockatt, Director of MI9, and paid a visit to the Foreign Office's Greek Section. By late January 1944 steps were being taken to secure Macaskie, now promoted to the rank of Acting Major, a place on a parachute training course at RAF Ramat David, in modern day Israel. On 29 January the Officer Commanding N Section was notified that Frank had passed No 94 Initial Parachute Course, along with another 'A' Force officer, Lieutenant Slatery and a number of American OSS operatives. At this point there was much debate about whether or not the military advantage of sending him back to

Greece would outweigh the personal risk that he would run. The British Embassy to Greece was pressing for him to be returned to Athens in plain clothes, to assist in negotiating a truce between communist and conservative guerrillas, and to get those resistance forces in Greece to agree to work with the Greek government in exile in Cairo. Brigadier Dudley Clarke however was of the opinion that the Germans would be fully aware of his history, having probably taken over his file from the Italians, and made it abundantly clear in a secret memo that he was not prepared to see Macaskie risk his life to save the face of the Foreign Office, who in his opinion had made a mess of things in Greece, and to get King George II restored to the Greek throne when a large part of the Greek population opposed such a move. With the conclusion of a truce – the Plaka Agreement – however this need was obviated, and Lieutenant Colonel Tony Simonds now pressed for him to be sent back on MI9 duties, writing:

> As things now are, I urgently require to send Macaskie to the Main Force 133 Headquarters in Greece to be in charge of escape work in the rural areas … He will be attached to the Main Force 133 Mission and live with them and be under the orders of the Senior Officer for the Mission for all matters not affecting escape work. He will of course be in uniform and to all outward appearance be the same as any other typical Force 133 officer or other rank in Greece … His work will not take him into any town or German occupied area, and of course he will be at all times in uniform.[3]

SOE and the Allied Military Mission (AMM) were now operating in all districts of Greece, and under international law were to be considered combatants if captured. Simonds however still considered it to be prudent that Macaskie should perhaps go back using a false name and identity, as the risk of him being captured could not entirely be eliminated. The large number of escapers and evaders now at large in Greece, mostly highly important aircrew personnel, made it imperative to organise them and route them to the coast for evacuation. For the past year, MI9 had been utilising SOE's Force 133 Missions and their wireless sets to conduct this work, but it had not met with a great deal of success. Although these personnel were willing to assist, it was not their primary job. There was also the security risk of using Force 133 rendezvous points and caiques (used for bringing in arms and supplies) for evacuating evaders, rather than the MI9 equivalents with which Force 133 were not familiar. Simonds felt that Macaskie was the ideal choice for this job. His knowledge of Greece and the Greek people, coupled with the fact that he got on well with Force 133 and was also an escaper, made him the obvious candidate. It was important to have someone in charge of this work from 'A' Force, who not only could do it better than anyone else but whose considerable experience would earn him the respect of Force 133 personnel on the ground. Simonds added: 'Macaskie himself is extremely anxious to do the job and in fact spends his entire time asking when he can go in to do this work. He has quite got over his 'political minded' attitude, and there is no ulterior motive of dealing with politics.'[4]

Having argued and won their case against the Foreign Office sending Macaskie back to Greece, it now might have reflected poorly if MI9 were seen to be doing exactly the same thing, albeit under different circumstances, and a delicate political line had to be walked here. Reginald Leeper, the British ambassador, was however appreciative of the difference between sending an officer in plain clothes to German-controlled Athens, and sending the same officer in uniform to an established British force in the mountains. As a precaution, however, Macaskie was indeed provided with a new identity for his forthcoming mission. He was now to be known as Major William Anthony Parkes, of the Parachute Regiment, and was issued with a new service number and new identity discs. He had been instructed in the use of MI9's Code No.6, and his codeword for transmitting was 'Mary'. His codename was changed from 'Felix' to 'Byron'. His next of kin had also been informed of his change of identity. He parachuted into Greece in late May 1944, and was later to say that this was his most difficult moment of the war. Sometime later he described 'that feeling of being suspended in mid-air, not knowing what you will find on the ground'.[5]

In fact, he was dropped in darkness a long way short of the intended landing ground, from about 3,500 feet, and landed in a tree halfway down a mountain. He acknowledged afterwards that it was fortunate that the tree was there, otherwise he might well have rolled down the slope and sustained serious injury. He made his way to the British operating base codenamed 'Mortlake' (Metsovo), headquarters of the Allied Military Mission to the Greek resistance. Here, he met with Nicholas

Hammond, an SOE officer and commander of the AMM. Hammond in his memoirs remembered that Cairo had sent a man named John Close to be his assistant. He was good natured but not really up to the task. However in May:

> He was joined by Walter Parks [*sic*] who was a member of the A Force which was organising the escape of prisoners of war. Cairo sent instructions specifying that Parks should not risk capture, as he had already been caught twice and escaped. I didn't ask for any more information about him then, and learned his story much later … he had now returned to Greece with the double purpose of arranging a safe passage for escaped prisoners of war and of being ready to go to Athens immediately after liberation … when he first came to me, I didn't know his story at all. Three Polish officers arrived with Close and Parks. Their job was to find the Greek links of an underground network that led from Poland across Europe to Athens. When they found it, they could send messages via runners to the Polish resistance from Greece in about fourteen days.[6]

On 9 June 'Parkes' prepared his first report which discussed the method by which he proposed to get the Rams (codeword for shot down American airmen) out of the country. The report included information on the likely areas in which the airmen might come down, and the quickest routes for getting them out of Greece; many of the bailed-out crewmen were likely to come from aircraft damaged on raids to Romania (particularly the Ploesti oilfields there) and Bulgaria. Escape routes from the north of the country would be wise to avoid Thessaloniki, which was still strongly garrisoned by the enemy. The British agents were greatly assisted in their work by the fact that most of the countryside was covered – at least visually – by *Andarte* (resistance) bands and friendly peasants, who usually undertook the first part of the job by guiding evaders to the nearest mission station. Of more interest than the report is the covering letter which Parkes, as he now was, wrote to Simonds. This was much more personal and in it he states:

> I suspect that you may smell a rat in my proposal to remain in the south for the moment and may imagine that I intend to go near Athens. This, I assure you had not entered my head, and there is no need for you to repeat your reiterated order that I must keep away from there. Nor need you have any anxieties about my taking unnecessary risks. I need hardly say that I have no more desire to fall into the enemy's hands again than you have to hear of my capture. Incidentally I am growing rather a fine beard and moustache which will very soon quite disguise my face.[7]

All journeys had to be made on foot and the distances involved were hard to appreciate just by looking at a map. The terrain was extremely mountainous and a journey of any distance was likely to include at least one or even two 5,000-foot climbs. He reported that there was more organisational work to be done there than he had previously supposed, and it more than justified sending an officer, something which had been a matter of debate prior to the mission. He concluded with another personal comment:

> I am as happy as a sandboy. As you know I love the country and the people and enjoy being here immensely. The comparative hardness of the life suits me better than the fleshpots of Cairo. It is good to get really fit again and to be so physically tired after a fifteen hour walk, or rather climb, over the mountains that one can go to sleep quite happily in a bush.[8]

'Parkes' accompanied Hammond and the two Poles on a journey to Galaxidi, to visit an American station. From Viniani they crossed Agrofikoto high up above Karpenissi. Hammond was travelling much faster than the others and reached the village first. He had to secure the release of an unfortunate woman who had been caught and tortured by communist ELAS partisans under the false accusation that she collaborated with their EKKA rivals. Apparently, she was considered pro-British because she had sheltered a mission officer, but Hammond persuaded them to free her, the word of a British officer for the time being still carrying some weight. From Karpenissi they followed a high mountain range covered with beech forests for a day, before dropping down and staying with a Greek family, and then moving on to Lidoriki. Finally they reached the station run by Joe, the American officer. On another occasion 'Parkes' accompanied Hammond in crossing the country, visiting outposts and avoiding German patrols. The latter remembered:

> When we left Galaxorini we wanted to take Parks to Agoriani, to Parnassos, where we had a small station. As we would be crossing the main road which connects Amphissa with Itea, I thought I would take Parks to see Delphi by moonlight, as he had never been there, but at the last minute we were told there were German patrols at Chrisso, near Delphi, so we went straight to Agoriani, where the station commander was an excellent sergeant who had attacked several German outposts in villages near Delphi. He confirmed the reports we had had from the general headquarters of ELAS about atrocities committed in villages near Delphi, by German troops, with the aim of retaliation. Some units had come from French Morocco. When the visit was over Parks and I returned in record time to Viniani. We did it in less than three days, and we arrived exhausted.[9]

One of the reasons that an 'A' Force officer was necessary on the ground was the ongoing rivalry between EDES and ELAS forces at the borders of their territories. Macaskie was confident that there would be no serious difficulties in passing evaders from one area to another, but paid a visit to the General Headquarters of ELAS all the same. In a later message he added that if there were difficulties later, he would go back and smooth them out – he also stated that the prestige of Britain in the country was still sufficiently high that a local protest on the part of a British officer would have an effect, perhaps having in mind the example of Hammond at Karpenissi.

In addition to the RAF and USAAF aircrew which he was evacuating, 'Parkes' managed to get a large number of Poles away who had been conscripted into the German army and who now wished to desert (indeed one of the Polish officers had been sent to him on attachment to try to convince more to join them). He was now also involved in evacuating parties of Russians who had also deserted from the German armed forces. He had nothing but praise for his fellow officer Jimmy Corfe who had done a very valuable job, and had received plaudits from all sides. Quite apart from putting in motion the machinery of evacuation, he had a great deal of administrative work to do in housing, feeding and controlling the groups whilst they were waiting to go – in some cases for nearly a month. Some idea of what they were up against comes from his next report:

> The Russians are an extremely tough crowd to handle and quite without discipline; and the prevention of murder when one of their number ran amok with a knife, and their removal in spite of their violent opposition from the village where they were causing trouble and in danger of catching typhoid to an olive grove some distance away are but two of the less difficult tasks Corfe had had to perform.[10]

He added however that now all was quiet again, this was one of the loveliest parts of Greece, and that he would be sorry to be on his travels again. By 27 June 1944 he was at Portia. The journey there had not been without incident, as it involved crossing the line into German territory and out again. This would usually be straightforward, but whilst at 'Kirkstone' the local Andartes had launched a raid against the Germans, which was a costly failure. Apparently it had been expected, and five of their number were killed as well as fifteen wounded. None of the planned demolitions had been carried out, and the Germans had been stirred into activity, the result being that when 'Parkes' had to cross the line the next night it was a lengthy business. He added: 'About half an hour after I arrived at "Trinket" a Hun destroyer turned up and started shelling the area! I seem to be a magnet for the bastards.'[11]

One of the remaining tasks for 'Parkes' was to establish a small 'A' Force stores dump at 'Kirkstone' comprising about ten sets of boots, socks, hard rations such as biscuits and tins of meat, and chocolate. This was because 'Kirkstone' had to be passed by anyone heading to the coast from inland, and airmen were upon first landing poorly shod for walking long distances in the Greek mountains. He asked for the supplies to be dropped by air, in containers clearly marked 'For A Force.' At the same time, he asked if the caiques which came in to pick up those being evacuated could bring in food supplies, instead of arriving empty, as these were always needed. Macaskie's American Rams were often evacuated by means of a 'feather plane', a light aircraft which was able to land on the makeshift airstrip that he had created in a potato and cabbage patch. In some cases, aircrew were back in Cairo within ten days of being shot down, and it is estimated that Macaskie helped some 250 soldiers and airmen to escape from Greece to the Middle East.

By 29 August he was of the opinion that now German forces in Rumania and Bulgaria had collapsed, Greece would be free within a month. He wondered what MI9's plans were for Jimmy Corfe and himself in this eventuality, and suggested that once the Germans had left Greece, his comrade should head north to Thessaloniki to set up an HQ there, whilst he went to Athens and did likewise. There was a hint at the inter-branch rivalry which existed in the British secret services when he suggested that it would be unfortunate and bad for the prestige of 'A' Force if there were not representatives in both cities as early as those of 'other departments'. The reply to this message exists in Macaskie's surviving MI9 file at the UK National Archives, and in it the 'A' Force operative is asked to stay in position until further orders are received, but at the same time he was notified that an officer named Major Alec Caridia was being sent out via Smyrna to Athens with a wireless set, and Macaskie was to join him when in position. Exactly what happened next is not documented in Macaskie's file, and in an extraordinary turn of events it would seem that in order to spare national embarrassment at the highest level, both at the time and in the Cold War era which immediately followed, documents were destroyed or suppressed both in the British records and in the Swiss Federal Archives in Bern.

The Bern archives however do contain information which appears to show that Macaskie was next involved in negotiations with the German occupiers in Athens, using a Swiss diplomat, Alfred Escher, as intermediary. On 30 September Escher received a letter carried by an emissary of Damaskinos. The letter, signed only with the initial M and rank of Major, informed

Escher that the sender – a British officer – was authorised by British high command in Cairo to undertake negotiations with responsible German authorities in Athens for the handover of the city. In the post-war years, this letter would mysteriously disappear from Swiss diplomatic archives. However, it is known from other documents that it requested that Escher set up a meeting with the German commanding officer, Hellmuth Felmy. Convinced of the good faith of the British, Escher went to the German general the same day and showed him the letter in question. Upon reading it, Felmy, who aligned himself with the 'official' doctrine of Berlin, categorically refused the very idea of a 'capitulation'. However, after listening to Escher, the German seemed to change his point of view. In the end, he agreed to start talks with the British, who seemed ready to make concessions. Time was running out, however, for a possible arrangement concerning the 'handover' of the Greek capital to Allied troops. When Felmy agreed in principle to the opening of negotiations, the Wehrmacht was on the verge of finalising its preparations for retreat, while German civilians had already received the order to leave Athens.

Still, Escher seemed fully satisfied with the interview. In the hours that followed, he went to Damaskinos to set up the rest of the operation. In the greatest secrecy, a messenger, who remains anonymous, was responsible for communicating Felmy's availability to begin discussions to the British. After various adventures, the messenger managed, on 2 October 1944, to establish contact with the British base at Villia. However, due to a German counter-offensive, the messenger was only able to report the British response a week later, on

9 October to be precise. This response – it must be emphasised – reflects a slight step back from Cairo's previous position: the British High Command now no longer wished to negotiate directly with the Germans, but wanted to submit a concrete proposal to Felmy, which he might accept or not.

When the German general learned of the British response, he confided to Escher that he was ready to study Cairo's proposals, while clearly specifying that he would refuse anything resembling an 'unconditional capitulation'. Aware of the German demands, Escher decided to go himself to British headquarters to meet Major Macaskie. After giving his consent, Felmy provided the Swiss diplomat with a pass to cross the front line. For his part, Damaskinos lent his car, also having Escher accompanied by a private driver, whose presence was necessary to be able to cross the territories controlled by the partisans.

Late in the evening of 10 October 1944, Escher arrived in the town of Megara, where the British headquarters were located. On his arrival, the Swiss official was warmly welcomed by Major Macaskie and a certain Major D., who hastened to establish a radio link with Cairo. This unnamed officer was almost certainly Major Derek Dodson of SOE, known as the 'Scottish Baby' on account of his youthful looks, though he was actually 24 years old. Dodson had parachuted in to Greece for the third time in August 1944 with orders to link up with Macaskie. A proposal was written jointly by Macaskie and Dodson, highlighting in particular:

> *Die sehr ernst zunehmende Gefahr einer kommunistischen Machtergreifung im Falle eines längeren Interregnums*

> *zwischen dem Abzug der Deutschen und der Ankunft der alliierten Truppen.* [This very serious danger of a communist seizure of power in the event of a long interregnum between the withdrawal of the Germans and the arrival of the Allied troops.][12]

However, because of the absence of General Wilson, who had temporarily left Cairo, the whole operation was delayed. On the morning of 11 October, Escher decided to go back to Athens, promising to return in case Macaskie had new information to communicate. Having barely reached the capital, the diplomat drew up a report to General Felmy, before learning that it was too late to conclude an agreement concerning Athens; it had just been declared an 'open city' by the Wehrmacht. There remained only one unknown: the fate of the port of Piraeus which the Germans were threatening to blow up along with all its electrical installations. In order to avoid the planned destruction of the port, Escher once again offered his services. In consultation with Hellmuth Felmy, the Swiss consul agreed to an arrangement: if he managed to obtain from the British a formal promise that no operation would be undertaken against the retreating Wehrmacht troops, the German general would give the order to cancel the destruction programme. In the event that a British negotiator was authorised to go to the capital, Felmy indicated that he was ready to have a radio telegraph set installed at Escher's home, to establish a connection with Cairo.

As the situation became more and more critical, the new plan was communicated to Macaskie, who remained awaiting a green light from British high command. This green light would never come. Macaskie meanwhile had seen ELAS guerillas slipping across the Thebes road, towards Athens, and without firing a shot at retreating German columns. To him it was obvious what they were planning:

> The information Frank Macaskie … had from Orestis, commander of the ELAS 2nd Division … was that ELAS units started to secretly move to Athens the night before the departure of the Germans. This information was later given by Macaskie to Brigadier Jellicoe. He had disembarked at Patra on 4 October with British commandos … from this information that was transmitted to the general headquarters it was obvious that ELAS would give the order for the 'Battle of Athens'.[13]

'Orestis', codenamed after a figure in Greek mythology, was Andreas Mountrichas, Kapetanios of the Attica-Biotia Headquarters of ELAS. He was described as no ordinary type of man. At various times a sailor, cinema commissionaire, and coffee-house waiter, he was now the commander of the ELAS Second Division; he was thought by some to be a man of spirit and charm, though Macaskie was not one of these. Indeed, he made no secret of his dislike of the communists generally, due to the mounting evidence that they had aims other than driving out the Germans. He commented: 'So long ago as early in 1943 I knew that they were using the Resistance as a cloak, and they showed their hand when they began their attacks on [Napoleon] Zervas. If Orestes had pulled his finger out none of the Germans left could have got away from Attica except by air.'[14]

Brigadier George Jellicoe, son of the British admiral of First World War fame, was serving in the Aegean in command of a squadron of the Special Boat Service. In numerous daring amphibious raids he had made a name for himself as a fearless and decisive commander. On 10 October Jellicoe's force, the first British unit to enter Greece since it fell to the Axis, arrived at Megara airfield, after having first captured the aerodrome at Araxos. Here on the following day he was joined by Macaskie, who persuaded him of the dangers that might result from a delay in British forces reaching Athens. Jellicoe was willing to lend him ten of his men, and this platoon set off across the mountains to try to infiltrate the capital whilst it was still held by the Germans. Leaving Megara that evening by boat they reached Scaramanga, where they rested, before crossing the high ground into the capital. Christos Zalokostas, one of the leaders of the resistance in Athens, knew Macaskie from his days in the city in 1941. He remembered that morning that one of his fellow leaders, Spyros Markezinis, met Macaskie and his commando band with a request from Lieutenant General Panagiotis Spiliotopoulos. In 1944, at the eve of the Germans' departure from Greece, Spiliotopoulos was appointed as the representative in Athens and its suburbs of the Allies' Middle East High Command, and was reluctant to share the glory of entering Athens with anyone not Greek:

> At 7 o'clock we learned how Kapsalis and Markezinis went to Peristeri to meet Major Macaskie, who was

> coming down with 12 English commandos. They really pulled a dirty trick on him over there. Good Macaskie had parachuted in to occupied Greece for the third time in May '44. Since then he had lived in Roumeli next to Captain Orestis, and watched the preparation of ELAS to occupy the capital. He said to Markezinis: 'For two days I was urging Orestes to beat the Nazis who were getting away, but he only cared about entering Athens. The Germans are pulling away to the north, the Elasites to the south, like people who part amicably and then each goes off to his work.' After seeing this and parting with Orestes, Macaskie crossed over to Corinth, met Brigadier Jellicoe, and persuaded him to give him a platoon, so that there might be an English detachment, even a small one, at Athens. However, Spiliotopoulos, who was notified of the presence of the 12 Britons in the suburbs, begged Macaskie not to bring them into town. He preferred to contain ELAS with the fairy tale of how large landing forces and an English fleet were coming.[15]

After being persuaded to leave his commandos in an olive grove, Macaskie reached Athens alone at 4 am on 12 October 1944. He changed into civilian clothes and went to the Archbishop's palace, carrying his uniform in a small suitcase. There the Archbishop and Georgakis greeted him warmly, and were delighted to hear that the hour of the liberation was at hand. Later that morning, 12 October 1944, some bewildered passers-by in Syntagma Square heard the approaching sound of advancing Germans. A Wehrmacht band marched down

Filellinon Street, turned right onto Othonos Street and headed towards the Monument to the Unknown Soldier. The time was 09.45 am. Felmy laid a wreath at the Monument and then handed over the keys to the city to the mayor Aggelos Georgatos, the same keys that had been handed over by an earlier mayor, Ambrosios Plytas, to Colonel Otto von Scheven on 27 April 1941. On the Holy Hill, the German flag had already been lowered and Felmy departed in his car for Kifissia. The time was now 10.30 am. As the last of the Germans were leaving, Jellicoe and another officer arrived in the city on borrowed bicycles. Macaskie was there to meet them, and introduced them to Damaskinos, before the Brigadier went to report to Spiliotopoulos. A famous photograph was taken on this occasion, showing Jellicoe, Damaskinos, Macaskie and Alexander Cameron 'Shan' Sedgwick, the correspondent of the *New York Times* who was a friend of Jellicoe. Enormous crowds now thronged the streets, while the bells tolled in unison. Macaskie and Damaskinos were watching events from the balcony of the palace when on the spur of the moment the archbishop urged him to put his military uniform back on, so that they could tour the streets. Macaskie was surprised, but went to his room to change, whilst the prelate's car was made ready. Then with the Greek flag on the radiator, and to the sound of church bells ringing, they toured the city, cheered by rapturous Athenians as they did so. So close did the people press that they actually broke one of the windows of the car. The Greeks knew that he had come to try to negotiate some form of political settlement, with the aid of Damaskinos, which would prevent the civil war that he had seen in the mountains spilling out on to the streets of Athens. A woman who was present, Ioanna Tsatsou, recorded in her journal:

> The people roar with excitement. 'Englishman' they shout and lift the car in their hands. They try to touch Macaskie, and he smiles lovingly at them, with all the immense love he has for Greece. When the Archbishop and Macaskie came out on the balcony on Dimocritou Street to greet them, the crowds cheered as if their hearts would burst. Such was the longing in the voice of the people.[16]

At noon that day, Frank Macaskie visited the distinguished Athenian lawyer and legal scholar Dimitrios Zepos, who he had first met in 1941, to congratulate him on the liberation. Then he had lunch with Damaskinos, at the house of his legal advisor Giannis Georgakis, at number 1 Dimokritou Street. Macaskie might have been the first British officer to reach Athens on 12 October, but others were secretly already there. After lunch, Macaskie went to find them and see what he could do to help. The most senior was Colonel L.F.R. Shepherd, who had a network of agents all over the city feeding information to him. Macaskie asked him what he could best do to assist him, and suggested that he might go to the Hasana aerodrome to try to prevent the Germans from destroying it. Shepherd agreed and so he set off with all speed, collecting his commando band from the olive grove. They reached the aerodrome at half past two that afternoon, but were too late, the Germans had already completed their demolition. The Germans were now destroying the harbour facilities at Piraeus, but were there in great strength, so Shepherd decided that Macaskie should take his men to the power station, to bolster the ELAS band who were holding it against the Germans. This they did and despite a fierce battle with the Germans this critical piece of infrastructure was saved.

On the evening of 13 October 1944, Escher and Damaskinos, accompanied by Major Macaskie, could only observe the columns of smoke rising from Piraeus: the Germans had just completed the planned destruction. A day before, Escher had learned, through the intermediary of a German officer, a certain Major von Rumohr, all the details concerning the parallel approaches of the Swede Emil Sandström. According to Escher's privileged informant, this delegate of the Swedish Red Cross would never have succeeded in convincing the Germans of the merits of the proposals made by the British, who would still have given a list of twenty-seven demands to the officers of the Reich. This list has also, it seems, not been discovered in any archive. The following month, Consul Escher submitted a report to his government on his activities. In it, he made the following comment:

> What were essentially the true intentions of the British high command in Cairo, which at first undoubtedly sought an understanding and appointed negotiators for this purpose, but at the last moment seemed to want to prevent the conclusion of an agreement, is not entirely clear to me and does not seem to have been entirely understandable to the two English officers [Macaskie and

> Dodson] with whom I had to deal. The only explanation I can think of would be that Cairo perhaps subsequently feared that an agreement with the Germans that did not correspond to the principle of unconditional surrender could be exploited for propaganda purposes by the enemy, and could have unpleasant repercussions among the Russian allies.[17]

Escher's hypothesis seems all the more plausible as the whole affair, which he refers to as 'changing of the guard', took place simultaneously or almost simultaneously with Churchill's official visit to Moscow. Given the Reich's interest in provoking discord within the Allies, we can indeed assume that the German propaganda services would not have failed to exploit the affair, if the British had not withdrawn from the proposed agreement at the last moment. This would explain the potential for embarrassment of the Westminster government, but what of that at Bern? A suggestion has been mooted by Swiss historians that an uncomfortable feeling existed at the highest levels of their diplomatic corps; they felt that during the war they had deviated from their much-vaunted neutrality, and had acted in concert with the British against the communists. In the 1950s, with the world polarised between the West and the nuclear-armed Soviet Union, they would not have wished this to be widely known.

The following day, the British 4th Parachute Brigade arrived in the city in strength. Their presence reinforced the authority of the new Greek government. For twenty-four hours Athens had hung by a thread, but to the Greeks, Macaskie and Jellicoe were symbols of British power – they knew that more troops could not be far away. The effect on the city was a stabilising one – ELAS had hesitated, and their moment had passed. On Saturday, 14 October at 10.30 am, a celebration began in the Metropolitan Cathedral to the enthusiastic applause of the crowd. At the end of the service, Archbishop Damaskinos showered those present with rose petals and laurel leaves. In a moving ceremony, Themistocles Sofoulis, a leading Greek politician and head of the Liberal Party, later Prime Minister of Greece, offered these in turn to Jellicoe and Macaskie.

It was around this time that Macaskie met a nurse of Greek ancestry called Mary Cawadias. (In fact, Macaskie also knew Mary's brother, through his MI9 work, for he was among those Greeks who had escaped from the German occupation, travelled to the Middle East and had been trained by the British.) In her memoir she recalls that she immediately fell in love with him. Indeed Cawadias (or Mary Henderson as she later became) recalled that all who knew Macaskie loved him:

> Tall, with a halo of fine golden hair, almost too handsome, very gentle with a quiet, caressing voice, he spoke a little halting Greek and never learnt very much. He had deep-set blue eyes, a shy stutter and a slight limp – the result of his war wound. But behind this saintly, romantic façade Frank was strong-willed, firm, self-sacrificing and heroically courageous. He always disregarded his safety to help others … that day, as the crowds gathered around the archbishop's car, they caught their first glimpse of a young Byronic figure in British uniform …

> But Frank was so reticent, so shy about his experiences. He only liked to talk about those who helped him – and always with such love and gratitude. When I first met him, it was at a party at our flat on liberation night. He was, I remember, carrying a mountain of army rations – tins of bully-beef, which to us was like caviar, butter, marmalade, jam, biscuits, Lee & Perrins sauce – all the things we had forgotten. On top of this pile of gifts there were two long-stemmed, sweet smelling tuberoses.[18]

At the end of the war, MI9 promised to track down every one of its helpers in Europe and reward them for aiding the Allies, and as early as August 1944 it had set up the Awards Bureau to operate in France, Belgium and Holland. The Allied Screening Commission (ASC) carried out the same work in Italy and Greece. The brief was to investigate, assess and pay out claims submitted by helpers of British and American evaders. The equivalent of millions of pounds was paid in compensation through these two organisations. In Greece it was often a dangerous job, verifying claims and distributing compensation in remote country places riven by civil war and infested with bandits, and several members of the ASC (G) were former members of the SAS specially chosen for the job. By order of Tony Simonds, from November 1944 Macaskie was placed temporarily in charge of the Athens office of the ASC (G), which had as its objective the awarding of decorations and financial aid to its collaborators, as well as the restoration of damages which they might have suffered. The office staff under his orders consisted of old acquaintances including

Majors Alec Caridia and Herbert Packer (previously Simonds' deputy).

Although it might be assumed that Macaskie would have been more concerned with administration, he in fact made at least one trip to the Peloponnese accompanied by Shan Sedgwick and Mary Cawadias as interpreter to look for and pay 'A' Force agents who had helped and hidden Allied forces. The trio took a jeep out into the countryside, Cawadias remembering that the evening air was perfumed by the scent of the mountain cistus, wild lavender and the frequent tufts of thyme. As darkness was falling and a large moon appeared, the bumpy stony road proved too much for the jeep and it began to protest. Spluttering and spitting, it came to an abrupt halt. Although Macaskie tried to start it up again, engines were not his strong suit, and despite his fiddling and twisting the jeep refused to start. There was nothing for it but to sleep in the fields and walk early the next morning to the nearest village in search of a garage or a mechanic. As the only woman, Cawadias took herself off to sleep alone under an olive tree. As she was falling asleep, Macaskie came over to her to cover her with his coat before kissing her gently like a child and walking away. With the breaking dawn of the next morning some villagers found them. A woman brought fresh water and fruit, whilst her husband scrambled under the jeep, eventually managing to get it to start. The trio waved to their saviours as they drove off again, having repaid them for their help in army rations and cigarettes. Soon they reached a village taverna, where the owner had hidden a British officer in a barrel which had held retsina until such time as he could get him away from the Germans. Cawadias remembered: 'Rather uneasily and haltingly Frank then broached the subject of payment, "I know we cannot p-pay you enough for what you have done or for what it m-meant to my c-country but is there a small thing – something we can give you?"'[19]

The perhaps surprising answer was tomato ketchup, to which the taverna owner was apparently very partial and of which they had some in the jeep, with a promise of more to follow.

Macaskie's association with Damaskinos was not yet at an end. After the occupation ended, the archbishop was proclaimed regent of Greece until a referendum could be held for the return of King George II from exile. He asked that Macaskie be officially appointed to his staff, as his liaison with the British Embassy. Harold Macmillan, the junior British minister in charge of Mediterranean affairs, met Damaskinos on 14 December 1944 and recorded his impression of him: 'I was impressed by the wide grasp of European politics, the good sense, humour, and courage of this ecclesiastic. He is willing to accept the regency, but realises the difficulties. He shares our view that there must be no reprisals and no counter-revolution'.[20]

The king of Greece however was opposed to the idea of a regency and used his friendship with Winston Churchill to turn the Prime Minister completely against Damaskinos, saying he was both a Communist and a Nazi collaborator. Based on what he had heard from the king, Churchill called Damaskinos a pestilent priest, and a survival from the Middle Ages. He feared that he might even facilitate a communist seizure of power.

Ultimately, however Churchill's visit to Athens at Christmas 1944 would convince the British Prime Minister that King George II could not return before a plebiscite had taken place, and that Damaskinos remained the best option as a stopgap until the king's fate was decided by the population, especially while Athens was turning into a battleground between the British and ELAS forces.

Attempts to disarm ELAS partisans had led to bloodshed, leading to an outbreak of violence in the city known as the Dekemvriana. Following this period of fighting, Churchill decided to visit Athens to assess the situation for himself. He landed at Kalamaki airfield and was driven out by armoured car to board HMS *Ajax*; this light cruiser anchored in the bay of Piraeus would be his secure base for the duration of his visit to Greece. Damaskinos, accompanied by Macaskie travelled to the warship, and Mary Cawadias recounts a story which can only have come from the latter – that when they arrived on board, with the archbishop resplendent in black robes, coal scuttle mitre and jewelled staff, the sailors were in the middle of a Christmas Eve fancy dress parade, and the band had just struck up a rousing rendition of *The First Noel*. The ship's complement celebrated Christmas in a big way that year, sailors were jubilant and perhaps had received an extra issue of grog, for they at first refused to believe that when he appeared on deck, Damaskinos was anything other than a very well disguised British tar. They marvelled at his 'costume', though the story of one sailor pulling at his beard to see if it would come off may be nothing more than Greek embroidery of an already amusing tale. Churchill first met Damaskinos on

Christmas Day 1944, aboard *Ajax*. After meeting the prelate, Churchill completely changed his view of him, writing: 'It was impossible to doubt that Damaskinos greatly feared the Communists' involvement in Greek affairs...Generally he impressed me with a good deal of confidence.'[21]

Macaskie was present at this meeting. On Boxing Day 1944, Churchill again met Damaskinos at the British Embassy and wrote, 'I was already convinced that he was the outstanding figure in the Greek turmoil'.[22]

The weather in Athens was freezing at this time and Churchill kept his coat on, whilst Damaskinos wrapped blankets round their knees, as the two foul-smelling paraffin heaters provided by the military offered little in the way of heat. The same day, Damaskinos chaired a conference aimed at a peaceful solution to the crisis, attended by members of both EAM and the Greek government. At the conference, it was agreed that King George II would not return at once as he wanted, Damaskinos would continue as Regent, the Prime Minister Georgios Papandreou would resign in favour of the anti-monarchist General Nikolaos Plastiras and a ceasefire would be proclaimed to end the fighting. On 3 January 1945, Damaskinos swore in a new government headed by Plastiras, which was described as wholly republican and moderately left-wing.

In early 1945, Frank Macaskie was appointed as liaison officer of the regent archbishop Damaskinos with the British Embassy, and the ambassador Reginald Leeper, at the personal request of the prelate. The reason given for this was the successful way in which he had fulfilled the role unofficially up that point. In order to be on a par with his other advisors, he was given the temporary local rank of Lieutenant Colonel. At the same time, he participated in a new organisation, the Anglo-Greek Information Service (AGIS), Ambassador Leeper's creation, which was headed by Colonel Kenneth Johnstone and aimed to counter international left-wing propaganda about imperialist British policy in Greece.

The war in the Greek Islands was not yet over, however and in May 1945, together with New Zealander John Redpath, Macaskie was planning an operation to rescue Allied airmen on the island of Rhodes, which was still held by the Germans. The last Axis victory of the Second World War came in the Aegean in 1943, when upon the collapse of Italy the Germans had seized Rhodes. The British had mounted an ill-prepared and half-hearted attempt to drive them out of the Greek Islands, but the Germans had local air superiority and the few British and South African Air Force squadrons involved were defeated, with numerous combat losses. A number of these men were known to be still held as prisoners on Rhodes. Redpath and Macaskie got as far as the island of Symi and were about to execute the plan when the garrison of Rhodes unconditionally surrendered, along with all German troops in the Dodecanese. Around this time, Macaskie's romantic relationship with Mary Cawadias came to an end. She remembered:

> I remember I saw quite a lot of Frank Macaskie at that time; he was a great friend of Shan's and often called at the flat. He always brought some precious - to us – tins of army rations and bunches of sweet smelling flowers for me – hyacinths, violets or sometimes tuberoses. I still

> remember their dizzy scent. Then one evening we had a dinner date and he was late ... when Frank eventually arrived we went out to a taverna for dinner. But that night he seemed to me to be ill at ease, more silent and serious than usual. Over dinner he often stared at me with his penetrating blue eyes – I have a fixation about blue eyes, no doubt because mine are brown – but Frank's were of the palest blue, rimmed with darker blue, and had a pool-like depth. He seemed to be not so much looking at me as through me; I waited for his words. 'Darling,' he finally said. 'I don't want you to be hurt. I love you but I am not in l-love with you. P-perhaps we should stop seeing each other?' I remember at the time this dissection of love was new to me – and I presumed it was very British, All I knew was that I loved Frank, warmly, totally – like a foreigner no doubt.[23]

Perhaps Frank had felt that if he was killed, he would not want Mary to suffer undue grief and it was better to end things this way. The German surrender removed that risk, but now Macaskie was busier than ever with his diplomatic duties. In September 1945 Damaskinos travelled to Britain for talks regarding the future of Greece. During his stay he was expected to meet with the exiled King George II regarding the planned plebiscite. The trip was to some degree organised by Macaskie, and the party made the journey in an RAF Avro York transport plane. During the visit, Macaskie was interviewed by the *Yorkshire Post*, in its report he is quoted as saying of Damaskinos:

> He is a great statesman, and the only man who can lead Greece towards its realisation of a Socialistic State. The Regent has a great affection for England. He has, in fact often been called an Anglo-maniac … the Greeks have a fanatical love for England. As part of the Greeks are Socialistic-minded – not Communistic, mind you – they have great hopes that through the Socialist government in England they will be able to establish a Socialist regime in Greece on the lines of Britain's present system.[24]

Among those who met the prelate at this time was the newly elected British Prime Minister Clement Attlee. The visit had two main purposes – Damaskinos wished firstly to consider the internal situation in Greece *vis a vis* the plebiscite. Republicans had pressed him to hold elections beforehand, but monarchists had opposed this. Secondly in international matters, he wanted to discuss revisions to Greece's borders with Albania and Bulgaria, and also her claims to the Dodecanese islands which had been in Italian hands since the Treaty of Ouchy in 1912. It was reported in the press that Britain was in agreement on all of these matters, and was determined to offer Greece all assistance within its power. On the Sunday of his visit Damaskinos made history by becoming the first head of the Greek Orthodox church to celebrate the Eucharist alongside the Archbishop of Canterbury, Dr Geoffrey Fisher, at Canterbury Cathedral. Again, Macaskie was at this service with him. The Regent made an impressive sight in his robes and golden mitre. Speaking through his interpreter, the Greek Ambassador, Damaskinos paid tribute to the manner in which

Britain had come to the assistance of Greece during the war, and the fact that the two countries had stood side by side in the defence of liberty.

In the afternoon, his friend Georgios Seferiades records in his journal that he and Macaskie went walking around the medieval streets of Canterbury, admiring the architecture. Career diplomat Seferiades – also known by his pen name as poet Seferis – had followed the Greek government into exile, only to return with it to Athens on 22 October 1944. He was one of the few civil servants to attend the conference convened by Churchill on Boxing Day and by late May 1945, had been appointed to the Regent's Political Bureau. In his capacity as a civil servant he worked closely with British Embassy personnel, some of whom he knew even before he went into exile, or subsequently got to know in the Middle East. He forged a close friendship with Macaskie at this time, which would last until the end of his life.

In the wake of his visit to Britain, Macaskie was back in Athens, and wrote on 5 October 1945 from the British Embassy to his old friend Lieutenant Colonel Bill Stewart of MI9. This was in connection with the work of Major Lang who had now taken over at the ASC (G). Macaskie wrote:

> I am afraid Bill, I hadn't a moment to spare in London to do anything about the A.S.C. In the thirteen days I was in England I could only spend a few hours even with my family, but since returning to Athens I have been encouraged to believe that things will go better with the A.S.C. First of all Rydon is coming here as boss of the

> show. I knew him in Italy during the war when he was in 'A' Force at Demi & I think he is first class. He is a regular soldier, has lots of drive and will take an interest in the job because he won't, being a regular, have his eye the whole time on his release date & UK.[25]

He went on to describe the ASC (G) as 'rotten', but added that Commander Wolfson had also been in Athens recently and experienced the bad feeling in the unit himself. Macaskie believed that Lang resented him even stepping into the building, and ended his letter by inviting Stewart to Athens, saying that the month of October was delightful there – provided of course that there was no revolution!

One of the main causes of his fallout with Lang was over Macaskie's recommendation of Mrs Titi Douka for an award. Lang had heard rumours that she was a high-class prostitute who consorted with Germans, and was responsible for the betrayal of British escapers. He had written privately to Simonds to tell him that he was blocking her award as recommended by Frank. In conjunction with Bill Stewart, in March 1946 Macaskie visited the British Correspondents Information Service in Athens. The organisation assured the two that there was no file on Mrs Douka, no black mark against her name, and indeed she was currently employed by a British department. In addition Macaskie had, it appears, been supported in his assertions by his comrade, New Zealander Warrant Officer John Redpath, though by now he was demobilised and back home. Like Macaskie he had been an evader and escaper in

Greece before working with MI9 in the Aegean, and had also been appointed to ASC (G) at the end of the war.

After six long years in the army, Macaskie would soon be demobilised himself. The temporary local rank that the army felt he should have during his time with Damaskinos would also now be rescinded. On 14 November 1946 War Substantive Captain (Temporary Lieutenant Colonel) Frank Macaskie relinquished his commission, and was granted the honorary rank of Major. His transition to the civilian world however would see him continue to be involved with the turbulent politics of post-war Greece. In the assertion of some, it would also see him continue his work in the murky world of intelligence, work which would be of growing importance as the Cold War intensified.

Chapter Six

Out of the Shadows?

The years after the end of the Second World War are those of Macaskie's career about which we know least. This of course was at the very beginning of the Cold War. The Greek Civil War, which started in earnest around this time and ran until 1949, was the earliest proxy engagement of this conflict, predating as it did the Korean War. The communist factions of the resistance fought in a renewed struggle against the Greek government, the latter supported initially by Britain. This bitter fighting left Greece four years behind the rest of Western Europe in recovering from the ravages of the Second World War; France, Italy and others had by contrast largely begun reconstruction in 1945 with aid granted under the Marshall Plan. Exactly what role Macaskie played in Greece at this time may never be fully known. It has been rumoured that he was still working under cover for British intelligence, but if that is so the full picture may never emerge, for MI6 as a rule does not ever reveal details of its operatives.

From the close of hostilities, Macaskie remained largely in Athens, as official advisor to Damaskinos. Georgios Seferiades, his firm friend, wrote later:

> We spent the years 1945 to end of 1947 very close together. This gave me the opportunity of realising that this very

> bold man, this man of action, possessed at the same time an incredible sensitivity, an extraordinary power of affection and sympathy. I was moved by the way he reacted to the critical times through which our country was passing, by the way he fretted when others were slow to grasp our problems. It was as if he were one of us. He possessed that very rare thing, the gift of devotion.[1]

There is evidence that in December 1945, Macaskie was still in communication with Rino Rossi, with whom he had first come into contact on Rhodes, albeit now through a third party, Captain Keith Butler of the British Embassy in Rome. It may well be that Macaskie felt somewhat indebted to Rossi, for the assistance that he had given to him whilst in captivity. Butler was writing following a meeting between Rossi and Georgios Exintaris, Greek politician and representative of Greece in Italy in 1945. This meeting was part of a process of restoring normal diplomatic relations between the Republic of Italy and the Kingdom of Greece. Following the meeting, on 22 December, Butler had asked Macaskie to intercede with Ioannis Sofianopoulos (Foreign Minister of Greece between 1945 and 1946) to get Rossi accepted under some diplomatic guise by the Greek government. Butler hoped that knowing Sofianopoulos very well, Macaskie could have spoken to him openly and with full frankness on the subject. Macaskie replied:

> For your private information I do not think that the Italians have any chance of having an accredited Diplomatic Representative in Greece until they have handed over the

> Dodecanese and paid in full the reparations requested by the Greeks, and these two matters I believe have to wait until the Peace Treaty with Italy is signed … Greek public opinion is not willing to accept tricks from the Italians until these two issues have been settled; since the current government also now does not have public opinion behind it, it is not likely to take such a step in this direction... In any case I will certainly speak to Sofianopoulos about Rossi and I ask you to tell Rossi that I will do this and whatever else I can possibly do. I leave it to you [Butler] to tell him or not my pessimistic views....[2]

In February 1946 Macaskie hosted former MI9 comrade Bill Stewart on a visit to Athens and they attended a party thrown by wartime resistance leader Napoleon Zervas. The party must have been quite a raucous one as Stewart later expressed surprise that he was in a fit state to fly back to Cairo the next morning. After the Second World War, Zervas founded the National Party of Greece and at the elections of 31 March 1946, he was elected as representative of the Ioannina district in the Hellenic Parliament, in which his party gained twenty-five seats. Later, he participated in Dimitrios Maximos' cabinet as Minister without portfolio, from 24 January to 23 February 1947, and afterwards as Minister for Public Order until 29 August 1947. The election produced a right-leaning government which was favourable towards the monarchy, and later that year a referendum endorsed the return of George II. However he would reign for only another year before his death, and was to be succeeded by his brother as King Paul.

In 1947, Macaskie left the service of Damaskinos, and replaced the leftist Geoffrey Hoare as the *Times* of London correspondent in Greece. He went back to London briefly to discuss the newspaper's stance on the country and its problems. In a letter of 2 May 1947, Macaskie wrote to the editor Robert Barrington-Ward, 'I remember almost your last words to me in London were that we should do something about the present Greek Government. So far in my messages I have not been critical of it, though there are many of its actions and measures that are ill-advised... I think until the American attitude towards it becomes clearer criticism would not be helpful.'[3]

On 30 May, Barrington-Ward, in reply to Macaskie's letter, wrote: 'your task is certainly delicate. There is no reason at all why you should not report Greek opinion from time to time, however strongly expressed. It will be your duty as a correspondent to do so. But you will be reporting as a detached observer.'[4]

We catch another glimpse of Frank, in Spring 1947. This time it is in a letter from Jane Macaskie, wife of his cousin who was then with British occupying forces in Berlin. She writes:

> Mrs Sprigge had just come back from Athens. Frank Macaskie is one of her dearest friends, it seems, and she says he has been offered to be the Greek correspondent of the *Times*, and as the Greek news has suddenly become much more interesting, she thinks he must have started.
>
> She told us how it fell out that the *Times* was so utterly E.L.A.S.-minded originally. Their correspondent

> Geoffrey Hoare was in love with a young woman who is a well-known communist, an English girl who lives in Athens and whose name I can't remember. She was practically the *Times* correspondent, but now they have found out the horrid truth and sacked him and given the job to Frank. If Frank would only pull up his socks and get into one of these Commissions and take an interest in his surroundings, there are all sorts of openings for a young man with real brains. ...[5]

Sylvia Sprigge was a journalist writing for the *Manchester Guardian*. She was described before the war as 'Young, dark-haired, ethereal, enthusiastic [with a] personal shyness.'[6]

Originally from Johannesburg, she was nine years older than Frank, both highly intelligent and well read; one wonders if there was a mutual attraction between her and the decorated officer. Frank had, after all, been attracted to an older woman before. Around this time, Macaskie also became friends with Mario Modiano, who was Jewish and a Greek citizen of Italian extraction; it was only the latter which had saved him from being deported to Auschwitz. Like Macaskie he had grown up with a background of journalism, his father having been proprietor and editor of a French language Jewish newspaper in Thessaloniki. As Greece descended into civil war, Modiano's father was recruited by Reuters as their correspondent. Mario remembered:

> I joined the army as an interpreter and took the rank of first lieutenant; and I worked with the British military

> mission which was instructing the newly recruited Greek army in all military manners. And I was an interpreter. And that lasted for about two years. After two years I came back and I had learned some vestiges of journalism from my father, because I would help him whenever I came on leave in Athens from my posting in Tripoli or Kalamata and I met a lot of foreign correspondents who were here covering the events then which were very important for the international public. When I was released from the army, the then *Times* correspondent Frank Macaskie, asked me if I would help him, by reading to him, translating the newspapers and keeping him informed of what was going on. That was how I entered journalism…[7]

In June and July 1947, the Greek government launched a rumour-campaign aimed at highlighting the international dimension of the Greek crisis, and justifying further arrests of its opponents. In early June, publicity was given to rumours that an 'international brigade' was being formed to come to the assistance of the guerrillas, and that communists recruited in France, Italy, Spain and Germany had already reached Greece's northern borders through a Yugoslavian port. On 2 June Macaskie reported in *The Times* that, though it was impossible to check the truth or the origin of such reports, their effect was to draw together all anti-Communists in Greece. His article concluded: 'Unity is nearer than at any time since Greece fought united against the Axis Powers in 1940–41.'[8]

On 26 July, the left-leaning *Manchester Guardian* wrote in an editorial. There is little doubt that General Zervas and other members of the Greek Government deliberately exaggerated the importance of the operations on the Albanian frontier in order to impress the Americans and perhaps, to justify the widespread arrests of "Communists", real and imagined, in Greece. No international brigade appeared.'[9]

Another story circulated in the British press was about an alleged 'plot' by communists – scheduled for 9 July – to commit sabotage and murder and provoke disorder in Athens and other Greek towns. On 8 July, the Greek Government had claimed that the 'plot' was connected with a communist threat to establish a separate government and was intended to show that the rebels were strong in the urban areas as well as the mountains. On this pretext, the police made mass arrests in all major cities and towns. Police and army units were ordered to stand by. On 10 July *The Times*, together with the *Manchester Guardian* and the *Daily Telegraph* published the 'plot' story. On 11 July, Macaskie's *Times* piece was quoted in the *Manchester Guardian* as stating that the arrests had reached a total number of more than 3,000. However, he added, 'any suspicions that the Greek Government has used the well-worn Eastern Europe technique of inventing an imaginary plot as an excuse for putting away political opponents appear to have been removed by the fact that only the extreme Left-wing has disapproved of yesterday's mass arrests.'[10]

A gulf was rapidly developing however between Macaskie on the ground in Greece and his editors in London, who refused to accept his outlook on events. On 18 July he wrote to them:

> … in order to give the presentation proper perspective I have emphasised the external danger to Greece and the efforts being made by her northern neighbours to incorporate Greek Macedonia, as a first step, into the Slav bloc; and because of this I have represented the communist element in Greece as a fifth-column rather than ordinary political opponents … I have stressed the fact that the situation has little to do with this or that Greek Government or party… From here it seems that we are back in the days of 1938; that Greek Macedonia is the Sudetenland and Greece the Czechoslovakia. It remains to be seen in Lake Success [temporary home of the United Nations]…whether we are going to have another Munich and appease the Russians, in which case Greece will be lost and the seeds will be sown for another war, or whether the Americans and ourselves will show the Russians that we are prepared to take action to prevent aggression against Greece – in which case I believe the Russians will draw back and we shall have peace.[11]

On 3 November 1947 in a simple ceremony in Athens the Greek government honoured Macaskie with its highest award for military service. When he was presented with the decoration, of which he had been first notified in May 1945, it is possible that one of those present was Mary Cawadias, as she was before she was married, for she was still in Athens. She was now Mary Barber, the wife of Steve Barber, an English newspaperman and Athens correspondent of the

News Chronicle. Mary was also now a fellow journalist, as she had accepted a job writing for the American *Time* magazine. The marriage was to be short lived however, and she described it later as a mistake. It seems that she was also still close to Macaskie, though in the small world of post-war Athens, all English-language reporters must have been on nodding terms at least. Another, American journalist George Polk, was shortly to be murdered, and Macaskie, it has been suggested, was in some way implicated in this.

Up to this point the United States had pursued a policy of neutrality in the Greek Civil War, though it was a neutrality characterised by hostility towards Great Britain, which the United States viewed as still having an agenda of imperialism. George Polk was an American journalist with a particular sympathy towards the communist side in the civil war, and had stated that he was going to interview the leaders of this faction. He was later found tied up and shot dead, his body washing up in Thessaloniki Bay. On 17 May 1948, following a briefing by Commander Gordon of the British Police Mission in Thessaloniki, Frank Macaskie filed a short piece for *The Times* of London: 'Polk is known to have expressed a desire to visit the headquarters of the Communist rebels, and some disinterested foreign experts believe that he may have done this and been murdered afterwards by Communists for reasons of security. The truth of the matter will probably never be known.'[12]

Some think that even in the chaotic situation in Greece at this time, for a reporter to conclude, one day after his colleague's body was pulled from the waters of the bay, that Polk's killer would never be found suggests that perhaps he knew more than he was letting on. Furthermore, Macaskie was alleged, by Polk's widow Rea to have been her husband's 'enemy'.[13] However, no evidence for this appears to have been produced either by Rea Polk at the time, or by journalists since. Polk's death was blamed by the communists on 'Monarcho-Fascist' forces, whilst the Greek Government maintained that he had been killed by the communists themselves in a 'false-flag' operation, so that they could blame the government, and thereby dissuade the United States from coming to its assistance. Certainly his death came at a pivotal moment in the Greek Civil War. In 1947, with the Truman Doctrine, President Harry S. Truman had declared that the United States would henceforth provide political, military and economic assistance to all democratic nations under threat from external or internal authoritarian forces. The Truman Doctrine effectively reorientated U.S. foreign policy, away from its usual stance of withdrawal from regional conflicts not directly involving the United States, to one of possible intervention in foreign wars. This was particularly true if a foreign government faced an internal uprising that was communist in nature. Britain, exhausted and bankrupt at the end of the war, could now no longer support the Greek government, but at the same time the US began to provide money and equipment. Crucially it was of better quality and more plentiful than British aid, and it turned the tide against the communists.

Frank personally was not out of danger. The ongoing civil war raged around him, and as if to underscore this point in July 1948 he was at a party held in honour of the Olympic torch relay race, leading up to the London games that year. His group consisted of Lieutenant Colonel Casey of the British Mission to Greece, Mr John Roler, Second Secretary to the British Embassy in Athens, and Mr Roler's wife, and they were being entertained in a taverna in Katakolon, western Greece, when they were attacked by guerillas. A policeman was killed when he shot out the lights to give the party an opportunity to take cover, but it was typical of Macaskie that he should take charge of the situation, and along with two Greeks, he swam out half a mile to the Royal Hellenic Navy destroyer *Hastings* (which was waiting to carry the Olympic torchbearer to Corfu), and returned with a landing party to drive the guerillas off.

Frank was soon back at his desk writing newspaper copy, but the rumours about the real reason he was in Greece refused to go away. Further hints at Macaskie's ongoing links with British intelligence come from American journalist Cyrus Sulzberger's published diaries. Under date 4 October 1949 he writes: 'I learned today that Frank Macaskie has a special assignment from the British intelligence service, aside from his job on the *Times* of London. The King and Queen are determined never to leave Greece in case of war and occupation. His assignment is to arrange for hiding them and moving them around underground'.[14]

It is not clear who Sulzberger learned this information from, though he was married to the sister of Alexis Ladas, and he was in Athens at the time that he wrote the entry. Furthermore, it has also been alleged that Sulzberger was in fact a CIA 'asset' himself. The story is given further credence by the fact that in later years it was stated Macaskie enjoyed 'to a remarkable degree' the confidence of King Paul and Queen Frederica of Greece. He accompanied them on many journeys throughout the country and he 'came to be regarded as one to be consulted at times of crisis'.[15] A further piece in this puzzle was the fact that Frank's friend Shan Sedgwick of the *New York Times* was also related to Sulzberger by marriage. The previous year, 1948, Sulzberger had questioned British minister Hector McNeil about the propensity for British intelligence to use newspapermen as their agents, to which he is claimed to have replied, 'We only hire them in the Middle East.'[16]

A few months before his death, Macaskie wrote a letter to Georgios Seferiades, while the latter was serving as Counsellor to the Greek Embassy in London. This letter, which was in the possession of Mrs Maro Seferi, testifies to the warm relationship between the two men. The letter was sent from Primrose Ville, Horsforth, near Leeds, and was dated 18 July 1951:

> My dear George, please forgive this use of the machine [typewriter]. Unfortunately my right shoulder is still under repair and only its digits are in full use. What a joy it was to hear your voice this morning. Thank you for your concern and that vital difference between the fellow who intends to telephone or write a letter and never does so – I am included in that school – and the chap who uses the means of communication as their inventors meant them to be used. I believe that you belong to my own school of lethargy – or whatever you like to call it – and that is why I am grateful for your telephone call: it required an effort. With many family difficulties

> to sort out while I am at home, I do not propose to go southwards until the last possible moment. I shall have to be in *The Times*' office in mid-August for a day or so, preparatory for leaving for the 'patrida' [fatherland] once again. While in London I trust that we shall see much of each other. Do you remember two occasions which I associate with you so closely? The one when we were walking along Piccadilly and out of the kindness of your heart you bought me a sword-stick – which you could ill-afford, I am sure. The other memorable time was when we had the 'petit dîner intime' with Marina at the Ritz in Paris. It was apt that she should give you my telephone number. Kiss her on my behalf and accept through her, failing my presence, every good wish in the world.[17]

The post-war course of Frank Macaskie's life, and its end typifies the fate of a whole raft of young people, both Greek and British, for whom the daily danger of action, imprisonment, Axis courts-martial and the constant threat of execution, led to the philosophy of 'today I live, tomorrow I die,' and which affected their psyche so strongly that their subsequent adaptation to a calm and creative social life became impossible. Like the 'lost generation' which followed the First World War they were disorientated, wandering, and directionless. Macaskie had begun to drink heavily in the post-war years, perhaps as a form of anaesthetic, and in a short time was unrecognisable as the athletic hero of the MI9 days. He confessed to former resistance fighter and leader of a women's unit Fani Lampadariou that: 'Only another war can save me.'[18]

Macaskie's health however had also been permanently affected by his treatment at the hands of the Italians during his incarceration. In 1951 a specialist at the United Leeds Hospitals had written to his GP regarding his liver function: 'This patient has, as you know, signs of peripheral neuritis in addition to his hepatic fibrosis … I think that his liver damage must be, at least in part, related to his starvation in various Italian prisons during the war and I feel that he is probably entitled to a pension at least on the basis of aggravation.'[19]

The specialist recommended large doses of vitamin B1 and avoidance of alcohol, but matters were about to move in an unexpected direction. When the dispute between Britain and Egypt over the Suez Canal began in 1951, Macaskie asked to be sent by *The Times* as special correspondent to cover the rioting which had broken out. He was taken ill there, two weeks before Christmas, with Sandfly Fever – the journalists' journal *Newspaper World* reporting that he had been struck down by a sudden illness, and whilst he had been rushed to hospital, he was not said to be seriously unwell – for the disease in itself is not fatal. He was flown back to Britain however, where he died of complications in Middlesex Hospital, on 19 January 1952. His death certificate records Hepatitis as the actual cause of his death. He was aged just 39, and unmarried. His fellow escaper Francis Jones recorded that he 'Died as a result of his wartime privations. So passes a very brave and honourable man'.[20]

His friend Seferiades was more expansive and wrote: 'I have the impression that the wounds of [the war] never healed. That is why I shall always regard the friend we mourn as a delayed victim of the war, one of those many soldiers who fell long after the enemy had left the battlefield.'[21]

At his funeral at Rawdon, near Leeds, there were wreaths from the Greek Government, the Greek Ambassador in London, and members of the Greek Embassy staff. The Greek Minister Plenipotentiary in London, Alexander Pallis, attended in person. One cannot help but be struck by the parallels between a hero of one war, T.E. Lawrence, and that of another, Frank Macaskie. Both risked their lives behind enemy lines numerous times. Both were captured and suffered brutal and degrading treatment at the hands of the enemy. Both galvanised resistance movements among subject peoples, and in consequence played a pivotal role at a crucial time in their respective theatres of war. Finally, both returned to a post-war world in which they found it difficult to settle, and even harder to replace the sense of purpose that war had given them. Both died before their time, trying to escape their own demons in different ways.

Appendix I

Biographical details of the main Greek protagonists mentioned in the text

Adosidou, Besy (Αδοσίδου, Μπέσυ) Wife of Georgios Trypanis, she had served with the Red Cross on the Albanian front before joining her husband's resistance group.

Cawadias, Mary (Καββαδία, Μαίρη) Daughter of Professor A.P. Kavvadias, she was arrested by the Germans in Athens for suspected resistance work. She later married the journalist Stephen Barber and afterwards the British ambassador, Nicholas Henderson.

Chrysinis, Ilias (Χρυσίνης, Ηλίας) Boat captain involved with the Karagianni resistance group.

Douka, Titi (Δούκα, Τιτή) Athens woman who sheltered escaped British PoWs and evaders.

Dovas, Konstantinos (Δόβας, Κωνσταντίνος) Retired Greek army officer. During the war he led the *Omiros* resistance organisation. He later became a Lieutenant General and in 1961 interim Prime Minister of Greece.

Doxiadis, Konstantinos (Δοξιάδης, Κωνσταντίνος) Whilst only a corporal in the Greek army, during the Occupation he was chief of the resistance group *Hephaestus*. He later was a member of the Greek government.

Evert, Aggelos (Έβερτ, Άγγελος) Chief of the Athens police force, he gave the impression of supporting the occupying forces whilst secretly assisting the resistance.

Exintaris, Georgios (Εξηντάρης, Γεώργιος) Diplomat and politician with a special interest in Italian matters, in 1950 he became Greek Ambassador to Italy.

Georgakis, Giannis (Γεωργάκης, Γιάννης) Lawyer and legal adviser to Archbishop Damaskinos.

Georgatos, Aggelos (Γεωργάτος, Άγγελος) Mayor of Athens, he was appointed by the occupying forces and replaced on the day of Liberation.

Kafantaris, Georgios (Καφαντάρης, Γεώργιος) Politician and founder of the Greek Progressive Party, he held a post in the November 1945 government of Sofoulis.

Kanellopoulos, Panagiotis (Κανελλόπουλος, Παναγιώτης) Founder of the *Omiros* resistance group under the Occupation, he later served in the Greek government in exile. In 1945 he was briefly Prime Minister.

Karagianni, Lela (Καραγιάννη, Λέλα) Head of the resistance intelligence group *Bouboulina*. She was executed in September 1944 by the Germans.

Karagiannopoulos, Leonidas (Καραγιαννόπουλος, Λεωνίδας) Cobbler and secretary of the Vathi chapter of EAM, on Samos.

Katris, Konstantinos (Κατρής, Κωνσταντίνος) Member of the Trypanis resistance group during the Occupation.

Kitrilakis, Stylianos (Κιτριλάκης, Στυλιανός) Colonel in the Greek army and leader of the *Omiros* group, he became a Lieutenant General and Deputy Chief of Staff in the post-war Greek armed forces.

Kountouriotis, Theodoros (Κουντουριώτης, Θεόδωρος) Son of Greek admiral Pavlos Kountouriotis, he was also a naval officer. In Athens during the Occupation he collated and transmitted information to Noël Rees.

Kriekoukias, Alexandros (Κριεκούκιας, Αλέξανδρος) British agent sent by Noël Rees to Athens in 1941 to assist with the evacuation of escaped British PoWs and evaders.

Kyrou, Achilleas (Κύρου, Αχιλλέας) Journalist and editor of the Athens newspaper Estia.

Ladas, Alexis (Λάδος, Αλέξης) A student before the war, after his escape from captivity Ladas became captain of a Greek raiding schooner and after the war a professional writer.

Lambrakis, Grigorios (Λαμπράκης, Γρηγόριος) Greek athlete who became a resistance leader. He was also a pacifist and after the war became a peace protestor. He was later assassinated.

Lampadariou, Fani (Λαμπαδαρίου, Φανή) Founder member of *Spitha,* a purely female resistance group. After the war she was active in advertising and design.

Levidis, Alexandros (Λεβίδης, Αλέξανδρος) High ranking naval officer from an aristocratic family who founded the *Maleas* resistance group. He was later arrested by the Germans.

Maximos, Dimitrios (Μάξιμος, Δημήτριος) Senior banker who was Greek Foreign minister between the wars and who in 1947 became Prime Minister.

Mela, Natalia (Μελά, Ναταλία) Relative of Alexis Ladas.

Melas, Alexandros (Μελάς, Αλέξανδρος) Politician and soldier, leader of the *Zanna* resistance group.

Messinezis, Filippos (Μεσσινέζης, Φίλιππος) Greek army officer who fled Athens with Macaskie's party.

Mountrichas, Andreas (Μούντριχας, Ανδρέας) Senior commander in the *ELAS* resistance movement.

Pallis, Alexandros (Πάλλης, Αλέξανδρος) Greek Minister Plenipotentiary in London, 1950s.

Papamichael, Irenios (Παπαμιχαήλ, Ειρηναίος) Bishop of Samos and opponent of the Italian occupying forces.

Papandreou, Georgios (Παπανδρέου, Γεώργιος) Greek politician, and founder of the Democratic Socialist Party, he was republican in outlook but also anti-communist. He was Prime Minister of the Greek government in exile.

Papavassiliou, Elias (Παπαβασιλείου Ηλίας) Baker in Athens and member of the *Bouboulina* resistance group. Brother of Sotirios.

Papavassiliou, Sotirios (Παπαβασιλείου Σωτήριος) Baker in Athens and member of the *Bouboulina* resistance group. Brother of Elias.

Paspatis, Georgios (Πασπάτης Γεώργιος) Athenian student of English who was part of the Macaskie escape party. Later the lieutenant and skipper of an SOE caique with the Anglo-Hellenic Schooner Squadron.

Peltekis, Giannis (Πελτέκης Γιάννης) A member of the resistance organisation led by agent *Prometheus II*, when that group was destroyed by the Germans he founded the *Apollon* resistance group.

Plastiras, Nikolaos (Πλαστήρας Νικόλαος) Soldier and politician, after the Occupation he led the *EDES* resistance group, though he was in exile in Marseille. With the liberation and continued internal fighting he became Prime Minister as a unifying figure.

Seferi, Maro (Σεφέρη Μάρω) Wife of Georgios Seferis.

Seferis (Seferiadis) Georgios (Σεφέρης (Σεφεριάδης) Γεώργιος) Diplomat and poet, winner of a Nobel Prize for literature.

Sofoulis, Themistocles (Σοφούλης Θεμιστοκλής) Greek politician, and leader of the Liberal Party. He remained in Greece throughout the Occupation, and although he refused to join the resistance he was arrested by the Germans in May 1944.

Stambolis, Nikos (Σταμπολής Νίκος) Piraeus harbour vice-captain, and later an executive of the *Aliki* resistance group.

Synanidou, Danai (Συνανίδου Δανάη) Member of the staff of the Bishop of Samos, and covert envoy to resistance prisoners in Vathi.

Trypanis, Georgios (Τρυπάνης Γεώργιος) Cambridge University graduate and former manager of the Athens electric tram system. Husband of Besy Adosidou.

Tsatsos, Themistocles (Τσάτσος Θεμιστοκλής) Brother of Ioanna Tsatsou and member of the Greek resistance.

Tsatsou, Ioanna (Τσάτσου Ιωάννα) Diarist and member of the staff of Archbishop Damaskinos in Athens.

Tsellos, Epaminondas (Τσέλλος Επαμεινώνδας) Retired army officer and former government minister; leader of a resistance group.

Tsouderos, Emmanouil (Τσουδερός Εμμανουήλ) Greek Prime Minister in exile during the Occupation. He was ambivalent towards the resistance, and distrusted due to his support for King George II.

Valasakis, Evgenios (Βαλασάκης Ευγένιος) Royal Hellenic Navy commander, and leader of the *Maleas* resistance group.

Xydi, Ieta (Ξύδη Ιέτα) Member of the resistance who provided a safe house in Athens.

Zalokostas, Christos (Ζαλοκώστας Χρήστος) Greek industrialist and Olympic fencer. A reserve army officer, he founded a resistance group.

Zepos, Dimitrios (Ζέπος Δημήτριος) Athenian lawyer and resistance figure, later a member of the Greek government.

Zervas, Napoleon (Ζέρβας, Ναπολέων) A Greek army officer, during the Occupation he led the resistance group EDES. He was both anti-royalist and anti-communist.

Appendix II

Significant Greek Resistance Organisations

Aliki: derived from the Maleas group. Under Captain Alexandros Levidis, it co-operated with MI9 to aid the escape of Allied personnel from Greece.

Apollo: founded by Giannis Peltekis under the direction of SOE. Apollo became one of the largest intelligence organizations in wartime Europe, with over 500 agents.

Bouboulina: founded on 10 May 1941 by Lela Karagianni and her family and named after Laskarina Bouboulina, a heroine of the Greek War of Independence. Initially, the group focused on helping Allied soldiers to flee to the Middle East.

EAM/ELAS: the National Liberation Front and its armed guerrilla wing; formed from an alliance of several leftist parties, it was controlled by the Communist Party of Greece.

EDES: National Republican Greek League; a right of centre organisation, some of its elements collaborated with the Nazis.

EKKA: National and Social Liberation; another right of centre organisation, it was liquidated by ELAS in April 1944.

Maleas: initially focused on aiding the escape of British servicemen to the Middle East. In October 1942, the group was split in two: Maleas 1, under the control of ISLD (the cover name of MI6), carried on with the intelligence-gathering operations, while Maleas 2 continued to aid the escape of Allied personnel, in cooperation with MI9.

Omiros: founded in September 1941, and made contact with British intelligence in April 1942. Active in the wider Athens area.

Notes

Chapter One

1. *Yorkshire Post*, 10 October 1922
2. *Warwick and Warwickshire Advertiser*, 25 January 1952
3. G.N. Frykman and E.J. Hadley, *Warwick School – A History*, Isle of Wight 2014, p51
4. E.A. Nickson, *The Lytham Century*, Lytham St Annes 1987, p103

Chapter Two

1. *The Green Tiger*, Leicester, November 1940, p267
2. Middlebury College Vermont Special Collections, Harry Massey letters, 30 January 1941 (author's transcription)
3. Op cit 3 April 1941
4. Tom Marston, interview with author, 9 February 2001
5. Stan Seddon, interview with author, 7 January 2001
6. Jack Saunders, interview March 2003, courtesy of Second World War Experience Centre

Chapter Three

1. Middlebury College, Vermont Special Collections, Harry Massey letters, 1 July 1941 (author's transcription)
2. The National Archives (TNA) WO373/61
3. Massey letters, 18 September 1941 (author's transcription)
4. *The Green Tiger*, Leicester, February 1942, p171

5. Nicholas Rankin, *Churchill's Wizards: the British genius for deception 1914-1945*, London, 2008, p178
6. Rankin, p324
7. Tony Simonds unpublished draft memoir (Simonds family)
8. TNA WO208/3253
9. Op cit
10. Petros Makris-Staikos, *The English Consul*, Athens, 2011, p225 (author's translation)
11. Francis S. Jones, *Escape to Nowhere*, St Albans 1977, p62
12. Richard Capell, *Simionata*, London, 1946, p44

Chapter Four

1. Jones, p74
2. Capell, p45
3. Jones, p95
4. National Library of Scotland, Acc.13338/406 typescript draft Paspatis, *Dead Reckoning* p88
5. W. Byford-Jones, *The Greek Trilogy* London, 1946, p27
6. TNA WO 208/3391, Leigh to Young, 19 September 1942
7. TNA WO208/3391, Clarke to Simonds, 18 October 1942
8. TNA WO 208/3391, Isham to HQ A Force, 1 April 1943
9. Yiannis B Ioannidis, 'The Tradition of Rasos' in *The Priest – Biseptimal Journal of the Orthodox Clergy No. 14* Athens, 15 July 1958, pp. 462–464
10. TNA WO 208/3391 Wolfson to Young 22 December 1942
11. Capell, p44
12. Swiss Federal Archives E2200.28-02#1968/176#442* 22 March 1943 author's translation
13. Op cit, 9 April 1943
14. TNA WO208/3391, Thompson to Maunsell, 24 April 1943
15. Macaskie family archive letter, 10 June 1943
16. Francis S. Jones' papers

17. Op cit
18. Op cit
19. Swiss Federal Archives E2200.28-02#1968/176#442*, 10 July 1943, author's translation
20. Op cit
21. *Harper's Magazine*, New York, November 1964, p87
22. Capell, p48
23. Swiss Federal Archives E2200.28-02#1968/176#442*, 27 July 1943, author's translation
24. Vatican Archive 96_0095_48r
25. Macaskie family archive letter, 15 August 1943
26. *Yorkshire Evening Post*, 2 February 1952
27. Swiss Federal Archives E2200.28-02#1968/176#442*, 15 September 1943, author's translation
28. Ioanna Tsatsou *Pages from the Occupation* Athens, 1965, p115 (author's translation)
29. Capell, p69
30. TNA FO 371/37206 R10450. Letter to Denis Laskey
31. Op cit
32. Op cit
33. Op cit
34. Op cit
35. Op cit
36. Op cit

Chapter Five

1. TNA WO208/3407, Macaskie to Wolfson, 27 September 1943
2. TNA WO208/3407, Simonds to Clarke, 25 January 1944
3. TNA WO208/3407, Simonds to Clarke, 12 March 1944
4. Op cit
5. *The Times*, 1 February 1952
6. Nicholas Hammond, *With the Rebels* Athens, 1982, p153 (author's translation)

7. TNA WO208/3407, Macaskie to Simonds, 10 June 1944
8. Op cit
9. Hammond, p162 (author's translation)
10. TNA WO208/3407, Macaskie to Simonds, 26 June 1944
11. TNA WO208/3407, Macaskie to Simonds, 27 June 1944
12. Dario Gerardi, 'Athènes 1944: la mission secrète du consul Alfred Escher: un épisode d'avant-guerre froide?' *Swiss Historical Review Bâle*, vol. 54, 2004, pp146-157
13. Ioannis Manetas, *Sacred Squadron*, Athens, 1996, p189
14. Capell, p45
15. Christos Zalokostas, *The Chronicle of Slavery* Athens, 2011, p377 (author's translation)
16. Tsatsou, p187 (author's translation)
17. Gerardi, p155
18. Mary Henderson, *Xenia a Memoir* Leicester, 1991, p223
19. Henderson, p257
20. David Brewer, *Greece the Decade of War, Occupation, Resistance, and Civil War* London, 2016, p198
21. Brewer, p199
22. Winston Churchill, *The Second World War Triumph and Tragedy* London, 1953, p274
23. Henderson, p263
24. *Yorkshire Post*, 11 September 1945
25. TNA WO208/3407, Macaskie to Stewart, 5 October 1945

Chapter Six

1. *The Times*, 1 February 1952
2. Marcello Rinaldi, *Verso un'inevitabile Amicizia* (Doctoral dissertation in Political Studies, Sapienza University of Rome)
3. *The Times* archive, Macaskie to Barrington-Ward, 2 May 1947
4. *The Times* archive, Barrington-Ward to Macaskie, 30 May 1947

5. http://www.sophialambert.com/JaneMacaskiesBerlinletters 1946-48.htm
6. *Daily News* (London), 28 December 1939
7. Centropa Archive, Mario Modiano interview, 6 October 2005
8. *The Times*, 2 June 1947
9. *Manchester Guardian*, 26 July 1947
10. *Manchester Guardian*, 11 July 1947
11. *The Times* Archive, 18 July 1947
12. *The Times*, 17 May 1948
13. Kati Marton, *The Polk Conspiracy*, New York, 1990, p341
14. Cyrus Sulzberger, *A Long Row of Candles*, New York, 1969, p472
15. *The Times*, 21 January 1952
16. Sulzberger, p412
17. *The Amaranth – bulletin of the Modern Greek Studies programme*, Dept of Classics, University of Toronto, No.11 1988
18. Makris-Staikos, p726
19. Letter from Rex Tattershall to GP, 5 July 1951, Macaskie family archive
20. Jones, frontispiece
21. *Yorkshire Evening Post*, 2 February 1952

Bibliography

Brewer, David *Greece the Decade of War, Occupation, Resistance, and Civil War* London 2016

Byford-Jones, W. *The Greek Trilogy* London 1946

Capell, Richard *Simiomata: A Greek Notebook* London 1946

Churchill, Winston *The Second World War Triumph and Tragedy* London 1953

Foot, M.R.D. and Langley J.M. *MI9 Escape and Evasion 1939-45* London 1979

Frykman, G. N. and Hadley E.J. *Warwick School - a History* (2nd ed) Isle of Wight 2014

Gerardi, Dario 'Athènes 1944: la mission secrète du consul Alfred Escher. Un épisode d'avant-guerre froide?' in *Revue Suisse d'Histoire*, Bâle, vol. 54, 2004, pp. 146-157.

Hammond, Nicholas G.L. *With the Rebels* Athens 1982

Henderson, Mary *Xenia a Memoir* Leicester 1991

Hondros, John Louis *Occupation and Resistance: the Greek Agony 1941-44* New York 1983

Iatrides, John O. 'Rival Visions: The Government in Exile and the Resistance Movement April 1941-April 1944' in *Modern Greek Histories, Volume One,* Athens 2008

Ioannidis, Yiannis B. *The Tradition of Rasos* in *The Priest - Biseptimal Journal of the Orthodox Clergy No. 14* Athens 15 July 1958, pp. 462-464

Jellicoe, Nicholas *George Jellicoe, SAS and SBS Commander* Barnsley 2021

Jones, Francis S. *Escape to Nowhere* St Albans 1977

Karagiannis, George *The Church from the occupation to the Civil War* Athens 2001

Ladas, Alexis 'Waiting for the Firing Squad' in *Harper's Magazine* November 1959

McLeod, Graeme J. *Two Home Runs* Waikanae, New Zealand 2020

Makris-Staikos, Petros *The English Consul* Athens 2011

Marton, Kati *The Polk Conspiracy* New York 1990

Nickson, E.A. *The Lytham Century: A History of Royal Lytham & St Anne's Golf Club* Lytham St Annes 1987

Parish, Michael Woodbine *Aegean Adventures* Lewes 1993

Perrakis, Stylianos *The Improbable Heroine* Berlin 2022

Rankin, Nicholas *Churchill's Wizards: the British genius for deception 1914–1945* London 2008

Seferis, George *A Poet's Journal Days of 1945–1951* Cambridge, Mass. 1974

Sulzberger, Cyrus Leo *A Long Row of Candles: Memoirs and Diaries, 1934–1954* New York 1969

Tsatsou, Ioanna *Pages from the Occupation* Athens 1965

Windmill, Lorna Almonds *British Achilles: The Story of George, 2nd Earl Jellicoe KBE DSO MC FRS 20th Century Soldier, Politician, Statesman* Barnsley 2008

Woodhouse, C.M. *Apple of Discord* Reston, Viginia 1985

Zalakostas, Christos *The Chronicle of Slavery* Athens 2011

Index

'A' Force, 37–9, 42, 46, 51, 97, 99, 131, 133, 138, 140–1, 154, 162
Adosidou, Besy, 35, 52, 64, 78, 91, 179, 183
Ajax, HMS, 156–7
Alexander, Harold, 38
'Aliki' resistance organisation, 50, 52, 117, 183, 185
Allied Military Mission, 128, 133–4
Allied Screening Commission, 153, 161–3
Anderson, G.G.B., 18, 33
Athens, 20, 27–8, 33–5, 41–6, 51–2, 54, 56, 59, 64–5, 76, 78, 80–1, 93, 99–100, 105, 107–108, 110, 112–13, 117–21, 123–6, 128, 130, 132, 134–6, 141–2, 144–7, 149, 151, 153, 156–7, 161–2, 164, 166–72, 174, 179–84, 186
Atkinson, John, 99, 108
Attlee, Clement, 160
Australian troops, 14, 16, 18, 22, 24, 51
Averoff prison, 111–12, 115, 117
Barrington-Ward, Robert, 167
Bavier, Charles-Edouard de, 99–100, 107–109
Bavier, Xavier de, 117
Bianco, Genetto, 94, 98
Black Watch, 25, 28
Butler, Keith, 165–6

Cairo, 10–12, 17–19, 21, 34, 36–38, 41–43, 48–50, 78, 90–1, 97, 99, 103, 120, 123, 125, 128, 130, 132, 135, 137, 140, 142–4, 150–1, 166
Canterbury, 160–1
Capell, Richard, 111
Carden, Donald S., 23
Caridia, Alec, 141, 154
Cawadias, Mary, 154–6, 158, 171, 179
Chrysanthos, Archbishop, 50, 121
Chrysinis, Ilias, 52, 56, 59–61, 77–8, 85, 89, 94, 110–11, 117
Churchill, Winston, 20, 129, 151, 155–7, 161
Clarke, Dudley, 37–9, 92, 131–2
Cold War, 141, 163–4
Collett, H.E.G., 26, 34, 37

Contra Spionaggio, 63, 76
Corfe, Jimmy, 139, 141
Cox, C.H.V., 18
Crete, 20–2, 27–8, 30, 37–9, 50
Crockatt, Norman, 92, 131

Damaskinos, 119–28, 131, 141–3, 148–50, 152, 155–7, 159–60, 163–64, 167, 180, 184
Dekemvriana, 156
Delphi, 138
Douka, Titi, 44, 162, 179
Dovas, Konstantinos, 45, 179
Doxiadis, Konstantinos, 50, 117, 180
Duca, Giovanni, 75

Eden, Anthony, 9, 103, 113, 128
EDES, 122, 128, 138, 183–5
ELAS, 122–4, 128–9, 137–8, 145, 147, 150–2, 156, 182, 185
Egypt, 9, 14, 18, 36, 47, 97, 100, 108, 177
Escher, Alfred, 141–4, 150–1
Evert, Aggelos, 52, 120, 121, 123, 126, 180
Exintaris, Georgios, 165, 180

Felmy, Hellmuth, 142–4, 148
Fernie, Tom, 5
Fisher, Geoffrey, 160
Fiume, 85
Freyberg, Bernard, 22, 27

Geloso, Carlo, 99, 107
Georgakis, Giannis, 119, 121–2, 147, 149, 180
Georgatos, Aggelos, 148, 180
George II, King of Greece, 49, 123, 127–8, 132, 155–7, 159, 166, 184
Gepp, Ernest, 92
Gestapo, 53, 54, 119
Gezira Sporting Club, 11, 19
Glen Parva Barracks, 8
Greece, 20, 22, 24, 28, 33–4, 37, 39, 43, 45–8, 50–2, 54, 59–60, 73, 78–9, 94, 99, 106, 108, 115, 120–9, 131–5, 139, 141, 143, 146–7, 149, 152–3, 155–6, 158–61, 163–75, 179, 183, 185
Greek Civil War, 124, 127–8, 148, 153, 164, 168, 172–3
Green Tiger, 9, 37

Hammond, Nicholas, 135, 137–8
Henderson, Mary, *see* Cawadias, Mary
Hitler, Adolf, 5, 14, 20
'Homer' resistance organization, 45–6, 50, 52

Italy, 14, 20, 96, 100, 103, 108, 112, 115, 117, 122, 153, 158, 162–6, 169, 180

Jellicoe, George, 145–8, 151–2

Jones, Francis, 52–3, 62–3, 65–6, 68–73, 76, 110, 177

Kafantaris, Georgios, 47–8, 180
Kallithea prison, 99, 100, 104, 108, 111
Kanellopoulos, Panagiotis, 48, 53, 180
Karagianni, Lela, 28, 35, 52, 179
Karagiannopoulos, Leonidas, 98, 180
Kaskinou Prison, 80–5
Katakolon, 174
Katris, Konstantinos, 35, 180
Kea 59, 66, 70–2, 74, 77
Kitrilakis, Stylianos 45–6, 181
Kountouriotis, Theodoros 45, 181
Kriekoukias, Alexandros 52, 181
Kythnos 60, 64, 67, 70–1, 73–4

Ladas, Alexis, 43–5, 47, 49, 52–3, 78, 81, 83–5, 94–5, 106–107, 110–12, 130, 174, 181–2
Lambrakis, Grigorios, 48, 50, 181
Laskey, Denis S., 127
Lavrio, 52, 56, 117, 120
Lawrence, T.E., 178
Leeds, 1–2, 5–6, 93, 175, 177–8
Leeds Daily News, 1
Leeper, Reginald, 134, 157–8
Leicestershire Regiment, 8–9, 13, 20, 37, 41
Levidis, Alexandros, 43, 45, 50, 181, 185
Lippett, John, 21
London, 5, 11, 92, 97, 105, 161, 167, 170, 172–6, 178, 182

MI6, 41, 164, 186
MI9, 37, 39, 41, 43, 78, 90, 92, 99, 129–34, 141, 152–3, 161, 163, 166, 176, 185–6
Macaskie, Audrey, 104, 130
Macaskie, Francis Cunningham, 1, 6
Macaskie, Jane, 167
Macaskie, John, 1, 42, 130
Macaskie, Nadine, 104, 105, 115–16
Macaskie, Thomas Septimus, 1
Magaldi, Gherardo, 107–10, 112
Malvern College, 12
Markham, A.R., 26, 35, 37
Markezinis, Spyros, 146–7
Marriott, John, 18, 32, 37
Marston, Tom, 23
Massey, Harry, 10, 12–13, 19, 30, 36, 42, 44
Maximos, Dimitrios, 166, 182
Megara, 143, 146
Mela, Natalia, 111, 182
Melas, Alexandros ('Alex'), 45, 182
Messinezis, Filippos, 52, 90, 182
Metsovo, 134
Military Cross, 33, 84, 130
Modiano, Mario, 168
Montgomery, Hugh, 102–103
Montrose Standard, 1

Moorlands School, 2
Mountrichas, Andreas, 145, 147, 182
Mussolini, Benito, 14, 112, 115

N Section, 39, 41, 104, 131
Natusch, Roy Spencer, 58, 62–3, 65–6, 68–71, 74, 79–80, 106
New York Times, 148, 175
New Zealand troops, 14, 22, 51, 58, 65, 77, 158, 162
Nicholls, A.W.D., 18
Northern Ireland, 8
Norway campaign, 8, 51

Oxford University, 5, 7, 89

Pallis, Alexander, 178, 182
Papamichael, Irenios, 94, 96–8, 182
Papavassiliou brothers, 28, 182
Parachute Regiment, 134
Paspatis, Alexander, 50, 52
Paspatis, Georgios, 52–3, 81–2, 85–6, 89–91, 182
Paul, King of Greece, 166, 175
Peltekis, Giannis, 46, 183, 185
Pignatelli, Antonio 99
Piraeus, 27–8, 46, 53–4, 61, 77, 99, 125–6, 144, 150, 156, 183
Plaka agreement, 128, 132
Plastiras, Nikolaos, 157, 183
Plytas, Ambrosios, 148
Preston, 6

Rangecroft, Rex, 10
Red Army, 129
Redpath, John, 158, 162
Rees, Noël, 29, 36, 40–2, 45, 47, 49–50, 78, 89, 92, 97–8, 104, 130, 181
Rhodes, 17, 75, 77, 80–2, 84–5, 93, 99, 118, 158, 165
Riding, George A., 2–3, 5
Roler, John, 174
Rolleston, Aideen, 3–4
Roncalli, Angelo Giuseppe, 101, 104
Rossi, Rino, 84–5, 118, 165–6
Royal Lytham and St Anne's Golf Club, 5–6
Royal Navy, 21, 30

Saros, 68
Saunders, Jack, 25–7
Seddon, Stan, 25
Sedgwick, Alexander Cameron 'Shan', 148, 154, 175
Seferiades, Georgios, 116, 161, 164, 175, 177
Shepherd, L.F.R., 149–50
Sidi Barani, 13–14, 18
Simonds, Tony, 39, 92–3, 97–8, 131–3, 136, 153–4, 162
Singapore, 76
Sofianopoulos, Ioannis, 165–6
Sofoulis, Themistocles, 47–8, 152, 180, 183
Special Air Service, 38, 153

Special Boat Service, 146
Special Operations Executive, 39, 45–6, 52, 133, 135, 143, 183, 185
Spiliotopoulos, Panagiotis, 146–8
Sprigge, Sylvia, 167–8
Stalin, Josef, 129
Stambolis, Nikos, 52, 183
Stewart, Bill, 161–2, 166
Synanidou, Danai, 94, 96, 98, 183
Symi, 158
Syros, 63, 74–5, 77

The Times, 167–70, 172, 174, 176–7
Thessaloniki, 50, 125, 136, 141, 168, 172
Thomashausen, Edgar, 35, 51, 118
Tobruk, 16, 18
Trypanis, Georgios, 28, 35, 43, 45, 51–3, 57, 64, 77, 81, 111, 117, 179–80, 183
Tsatsou, Ioanna, 119, 149, 184
Tsellos, Epameinondas, 45–6, 184
Tsouderos, Emmanouil, 49, 128, 184

United States, 12, 98, 131, 135, 137, 140, 153, 167, 170–4

Valasakis, Evgenios, 47, 49–50, 184
Vatican, 101–103, 113, 115
Vecchiarelli, Carlo, 107, 112
Vernicos, Emmanuele, 99
'Villa Marina' prison, *see* Kaskinou

Warwick School, 2–4
Wavell, Archibald, 14, 37
Wilson, Henry Maitland, 101–102, 144
Wolfson, Vladimir, 40, 42, 130, 162
Woodbine-Parish, Michael, 78, 90–1
Woodhouse, Christopher, 128

Xydi, Ieta, 35, 184

Yorkshire Evening News, 1
Yorkshire Post, 2, 159

Zalokostas, Christos, 146, 184
Zandonati, Rudolf de, 78
Zepos, Dimitrios, 149, 184
Zervas, Napoleon, 122, 145, 166, 169, 184